THiNK

STUDENT'S BOOK STARTER

Herbert Puchta, Jeff Stranks & Peter Lewis-Jones

CAMBRIDGE
UNIVERSITY PRESS

CONTENTS

PRONUNCIATION	THINK	SKILLS	
/h/ or /w/ in question words	**Values:** The Olympic Spirit **Self-esteem:** The 'Me' flag	Reading	Website: Mad about The Olympics Dialogue: Favourite football teams Photostory: Just a little joke
		Listening	Radio quiz: The One-Minute Challenge
		Writing	Completing a questionnaire: Personal information
Vowel sounds – adjectives	**Values:** Welcoming a new classmate **Train to Think:** Categorising	Reading	Text messages: Hi there! Dialogue: Deciding what to do Culture: Masks from around the world
		Listening	Dialogues: Talking about feelings
		Writing	Text message: Describing feelings and things
this / that / these / those	**Values:** Families **Self-esteem:** Being part of a family	Reading	Article: Kate Middleton Dialogue: Agata's family Photostory: A song for Ruby
		Listening	Dialogues: Describing family
		Writing	Description: Your favourite room
Word stress in numbers	**Values:** My town/city **Train to Think:** Exploring numbers	Reading	Brochure: Window of the World Dialogues: In the shops Culture: Parks around the world
		Listening	Dialogues: Asking for directions
		Writing	Brochure: A brochure for your town / city
Present simple verbs – third person	**Values:** Better together or better alone? **Self-esteem:** What makes me happy?	Reading	Newsletter: I love Glee club! Quiz: Does TV control your life? Photostory: The school play
		Listening	Monologues: Describing electronic gadgets
		Writing	Paragraph: Days in your life
Long vowel sound /eɪ/	**Values:** Helping a friend **Train to Think:** Attention to detail	Reading	Article: A real friend Dialogue: A surprise for Olivia Culture: Welcoming people around the world
		Listening	Interview: Friendship bands
		Writing	Paragraph: Describing a friend
Long vowel sound /ɔː/	**Values:** The importance of sport **Self-esteem:** My time cake	Reading	Article: They're good! Article: The Other Final Photostory: The big match
		Listening	Phone call: Making arrangements
		Writing	Paragraph: My favourite sportsperson
Intonation – listing items	**Values:** Music **Train to Think:** Memorising	Reading	Tweets: #musicinsupermarket Dialogue: A conversation at a party Culture: Musical instruments around the world
		Listening	Radio programme: Dances around the world
		Writing	Tweet: Describing a scene
Intonation – giving two choices	**Values:** How you eat is important. **Self-esteem:** You are what you eat.	Reading	Article: Young kitchen stars Menu and dialogue: In a restaurant Photostory: The pizza
		Listening	Dialogue: Cooking
		Writing	Menu: A meal plan for your friend
Past simple regular verbs	**Values:** Hard work and achievement **Train to Think:** Sequencing	Reading	Article: It was her dream to be an astronaut Article: Fictional heroes Culture: Statues
		Listening	Dialogue: Freddie's Saturday evening
		Writing	Proposal: A statue in my town
Past simple irregular verbs	**Values:** Animals and us **Self-esteem:** Animals and nature	Reading	Article: Erin and Tonk to the rescue Article: Extinct animals Photostory: The spider
		Listening	Dialogue: Becky's holiday
		Writing	Blog entry: A day in the life of an animal
Word stress – comparatives	**Values:** Transport and the environment **Train to Think:** Comparing	Reading	Article: The great race Article: My favourite journey Culture: Transport around the world
		Listening	Dialogue: At the train station
		Writing	Description: Unusual forms of transport

WELCOME

The alphabet

Aa Bb Cc Dd

Ee Ff Gg Hh

Ii Jj Kk Ll

Mm Nn Oo

Pp Qq Rr Ss

Tt Uu Vv Ww

Xx Yy Zz

1 🔊 1.02 Listen to the alphabet. Then listen again and repeat.

2 🔊 1.03 Listen to the sounds and repeat.

/eɪ/	/iː/	/e/	/aɪ/	/əʊ/	/uː/	/ɑː/
a h j k	b c d e g p t v	f l m n s x z	i y	o	q u w	r

3 **SPEAKING** Work in pairs. Spell your name to your partner. Your partner writes your name. Is he/she correct?

Colours

1 Write the colours in the correct places in the key.

black | blue | brown | green | grey | orange
pink | purple | red | ~~white~~ | yellow

Key

1 _white_   7 _____
2 _____ 8 _____
3 _____ 9 _____
4 _____ 10 _____
5 _____ 11 _____
6 _____

2 **SPEAKING** Work in pairs. What colours can you see around you? Tell your partner.

International words

1 Match the words in the list with the pictures. Write 1–16 in the boxes.

1 airport | 2 bus | 3 café
4 city | 5 football | 6 hamburger
7 hotel | 8 phone | 9 pizza
10 restaurant | 11 sandwich
12 sushi | 13 taxi | 14 television
15 tablet | 16 wi-fi

2 ◀))1.04 Listen, check and repeat.

3 SPEAKING Work in pairs. Choose one of the words in Exercise 1 and spell it to your partner. He/She writes the word. Is he/she correct?

5

Articles: *a* and *an*

1 Match the sentences in the list with the pictures. Write 1–4 in the boxes.

1 It's a blue football.

2 It's an orange football.

3 It's a red football.

4 It's a black and white football.

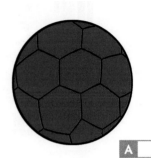

A ☐

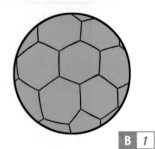

B ☐ 1

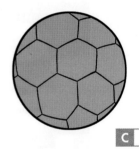

C ☐

D ☐

2 Write *a* or *an*.

0 *an* airport

1 _____ Italian restaurant

2 _____ red bus

3 _____ sandwich

4 _____ yellow taxi

5 _____ orange phone

6 _____ American football player

7 _____ famous actor

The day

1 Write the words in the list under the pictures.

afternoon | ~~evening~~ | morning | night

_____*evening*_____

_____

_____

_____

Saying *Hello* and *Goodbye*

1 🔊 1.05 **Complete the dialogues with the words in the list. Listen and check.**

Bye | Good | have | Hi | How | morning
night | See you | thanks | ~~this~~

1

ANDY   Hello. My name's Andy.

TOM   Hi, Andy. I'm Tom, and ⁰ _*this*_ is Lucy.

LUCY   ¹_____ , Andy.

ANDY   Hi, Tom. Hi, Lucy.

2

ABI   ²_____ afternoon, Mrs Hamilton.

MRS HAMILTON   Hi, Abi. ³_____ are you?

ABI   Great, ⁴_____ . And you?

MRS HAMILTON   I'm fine, thanks.

3

DAVE   Good ⁵_____ , Mr Thomas.

MR THOMAS   Hello, Dave. How are you?

DAVE   I'm fine, thank you.

MR THOMAS   Good. I'll see you in class.

DAVE   ⁶_____ , Mr Thomas.

4

JIM   Bye, Rachel.

RACHEL   Bye, Jim. ⁷_____ later.

JIM   Yeah, ⁸_____ a good day.

5

SUE   Good ⁹_____ , Mum.

MUM   Night, Sue. Sleep well.

Classroom objects

1 Look at the pictures. Do you know these words? If not, ask your teacher: *What's … in English?*

0 _____door_____   1 _____

2 _____   3 _____

4 _____   5 _____

6 _____   7 _____

8 _____   9 _____

2 🔊 1.06 Write the words in the list under the pictures in Exercise 1. Listen, check and repeat.

board | book | chair | computer | desk | ~~door~~ | pen | pencil | projector | window

3 Are there any other classroom objects you can think of?

4 SPEAKING Work in pairs. Point to the pictures in Exercise 1. Ask and answer questions.

> What's this in English?

> It's a desk.

5 SPEAKING Work in pairs. Find things in your classroom and say the colours.

> a red pen

> an orange chair

Numbers 0–20

1 🔊 1.07 Look at the numbers 0–20. Listen and repeat.

0	zero/'oh'		
1	one	11	eleven
2	two	12	twelve
3	three	13	thirteen
4	four	14	fourteen
5	five	15	fifteen
6	six	16	sixteen
7	seven	17	seventeen
8	eight	18	eighteen
9	nine	19	nineteen
10	ten	20	twenty

2 SPEAKING Work in pairs. Choose three numbers from Exercise 1. Tell a partner to write them. Is he/she right?

3 🔊 1.08 Listen and write the phone numbers you hear.

1 _____   3 _____

2 _____   4 _____

4 SPEAKING What's your favourite number? Compare with a partner.

Plural nouns

1 Write the words under the pictures.

0 _two chairs_   1 _____   2 _____

3 _____   4 _____   5 _____

2 Match the singular and plural nouns.

Singular		Plural	
0	one man	b	a	three people
1	one woman		b	four men
2	one person		c	six children
3	one child		d	five women

Classroom language

1 🔊 1.09 **Listen and number the phrases in the order you hear them. Write 1–10 in the boxes.**

☐ **a** Open your books.

☐ **c** Put your hand up.

☐ **e** What does this mean?

☐ **g** That's right.

1 **i** Close your books.

2 🔊 1.10 **Listen again and repeat.**

☐ **b** Listen!

☐ **d** Look at the picture.

☐ **f** Sorry, I don't understand.

☐ **h** That's wrong.

☐ **j** Work with a partner.

Numbers 20–100

1 🔊 **1.11** **Match the numbers with the words. Listen and check.**

a 20
b 30
c 40
d 50
e 60
f 70
g 80
h 90
i 100

	fifty
	eighty
	ninety
	seventy
	one hundred
	thirty
a	twenty
	sixty
	forty

> **LOOK!**
> 33 = thirty-three   56 = fifty-six   97 = ninety-seven

2 🔊 **1.12** **How do you say these numbers? Listen, check and repeat.**

1	24	4	49	7	74
2	87	5	54	8	95
3	33	6	62		

3 **Write the numbers.**

0	24	_twenty-four_
1	47	_____
2	60	_____
3	89	_____
4	30	_____
5	58	_____
6	72	_____
7	91	_____

Messages

1 🔊 **1.13** **Read and listen to the message. Complete the message to Liam.**

Hi, Liam,

Message from Oliver Holmes.

His house number is ¹_____.

The bus number is ²_____.

His phone number is ³_____.

2 🔊 **1.14** **Now listen and complete the message to Abi.**

Hi, Abi,

Message from Mrs Davis.

Her house number is ¹_____.

The bus number is ²_____.

Her telephone number is ³_____.

Review

1 ◀) 1.15 **Work in groups. Play the first letter game.**
- Listen to the letter of the alphabet.
- How many examples can you find for each category in the table?
- You get one point for each correct answer. The winner is the group with the most points.

	0 _p_	1 ___	2 ___	3 ___	4 ___	5 ___
Colour	pink purple					
Actor	Penelope Cruz Peter Jackson					
Classroom object	pen pencil					
Number (0–20)	—					
International word	pizza phone					
Total Points	8					

2 **Complete the words with the missing vowels and then write them in the correct column in the table below.**

0 f _o_ _o_ tb _a_ ll
1 d _ _ _ r
2 r _ st _ _ _ r _ nt
3 _ r _ ng _
4 p _ n
5 n _ n _

6 ch _ _ _ r
7 f _ v _
8 y _ ll _ w
9 _ _ rp _ rt
10 gr _ _ _ n
11 _ _ ght

International words	Colours	Numbers	Classroom objects
football			

3 SPEAKING **Work in pairs. Choose three pictures and spell the words for your partner to write. Is he/she correct?**

4 **Put the dialogues in order. Write 1–3 and 1–4 in the boxes.**

1

	JIM	Great, thanks. And you?
_1_	JIM	Good morning, Fred.
	FRED	I'm fine, thanks.
	FRED	Hi, Jim. How are you?

2

	LUCY	Yeah, have a good day.
	LUCY	Bye, Sara.
	SARA	Bye, Lucy. See you later.

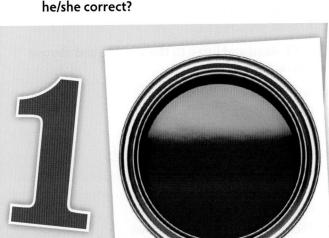

OBJECTIVES

FUNCTIONS: getting to know someone; talking about yourself and others

GRAMMAR: question words; the verb *to be*

VOCABULARY: countries and nationalities; adjectives

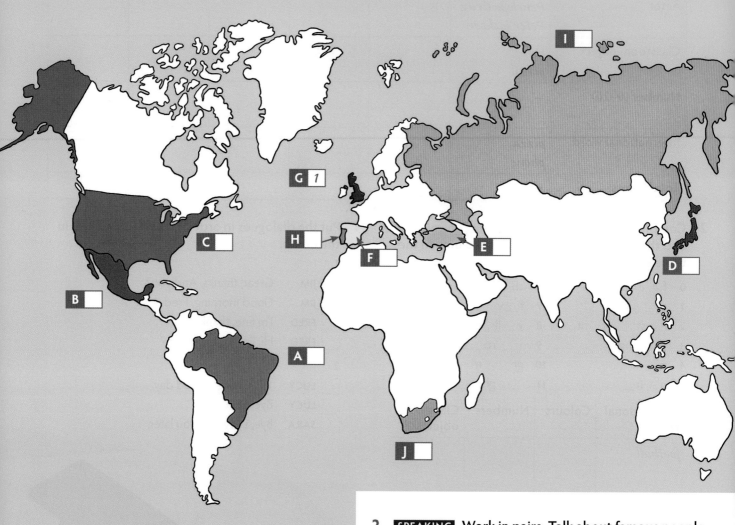

2 **SPEAKING** Work in pairs. Talk about famous people from different countries.

> *Neymar is from Brazil.*

READING

1 Match the names of the countries with the places on the map. Write 1–10 in the boxes.

1	the UK	6	Brazil
2	Mexico	7	Portugal
3	the USA	8	Japan
4	Spain	9	Turkey
5	Russia	10	South Africa

3 ◀ 1.16 Read and listen to the website and choose the correct words.

0 Pedro is from (Brazil) / the USA.

1 Pedro is *10 / 11*.

2 Brittany is from *London / Manchester*.

3 Missy Franklin is a *swimmer / runner*.

4 Oleg is *Portuguese / Russian*.

5 Oleg is *11 / 12*.

6 Haruka is from *Japan / the UK*.

7 Zheng Jie is a *runner / tennis player*.

Mad about the Olympics

HOME ABOUT NEWS CONTACT

Tell us about your Olympic favourites!

What's your name?
Pedro.

Where are you from?
I'm Brazilian. I'm from a city called Belo Horizonte.

How old are you?
I'm 10.

Who's your favourite athlete?
Usain Bolt.

Why is he/she your favourite athlete?
Because he's amazing!

What's your name?
My name is Brittany.

Where are you from?
I'm British. I'm from Manchester.

How old are you?
I'm 12.

Who's your favourite athlete?
My favourite athlete is Missy Franklin. She's a swimmer.

Why is he/she your favourite athlete?
Because she's great!

What's your name?
I'm Oleg.

Where are you from?
I'm from Russia. I live in Moscow.

How old are you?
I'm 11.

Who's your favourite athlete?
Mariya Savinova. She's a runner.

Why is he/she your favourite athlete?
Because she's fast!

What's your name?
My name is Haruka.

Where are you from?
I'm Japanese. I'm from Tokyo.

How old are you?
I'm 11.

Who's your favourite athlete?
Zheng Jie. She's a tennis player from China.

Why is he/she your favourite athlete?
Because she's awesome!

THiNK VALUES

The Olympic Spirit

Choose a slogan for the website.

☐ One world together.

☐ Exercise is fun.

☐ Win, win, win!

VOCABULARY
Countries and nationalities

1 [🔊 1.17] **Write the country under the flag. Listen and check.**

Brazil | Japan | Mexico | Portugal | ~~Russia~~
South Africa | Spain | the UK | the USA | Turkey

0 _____Russia_____

1 _____

2 _____

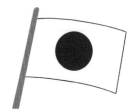

3 _____

4 _____

5 _____

6 _____

7 _____

8 _____

9 _____

2 **Look at Exercise 1. Complete the table with the nationalities of the countries.**

-an	-ish	-ese
	Spanish	

3 **SPEAKING** **Work in pairs. Describe a flag to your partner. He/She guesses which it is.**

> This flag is red and blue.

> Is it the Russian flag?

> Yes, it is!

Workbook page 13

GRAMMAR
Question words

1 **Look at the website on page 13 and complete the questions with the words in the list. Then choose the correct words to complete the rule.**

How | ~~What~~ | Where | Who | Why

0 ___What___ 's your name?
1 _____ are you from?
2 _____ old are you?
3 _____ 's your favourite athlete?
4 _____ is he/she your favourite athlete?

> **RULE:** *How*, *Who*, *Where*, *What* and *Why* are
> [1]*question* / *because* words.
> We often use the word [2]*question* / *because* to
> answer a **Why** question.

2 **Choose the correct words.**

0 (*How*)/ *Why* old is your best friend?
1 *What* / *Where* is your mother from?
2 *How's* / *What's* your favourite colour?
3 *Where* / *Who* is your favourite pop star?
4 *Why* / *Where* is he/she your favourite pop star?

3 **SPEAKING** **Work in pairs. Ask and answer the questions in Exercises 1 and 2.**

> What's your name?

> My name is Belena.

Workbook page 10

> ### Pronunciation
> **/h/ or /w/ in question words**
> **Go to page 120.** 🔊

LISTENING

1   Work in pairs. Look at the photos and tick (✓) the correct flag for each photo.

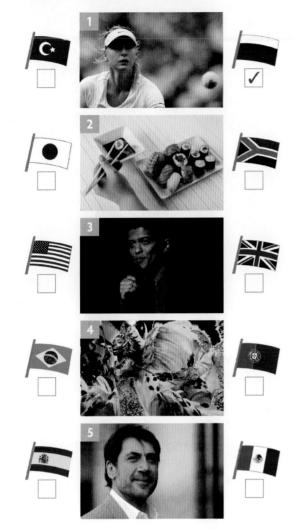

2   ◀ 1.20 **Listen to a radio quiz called *One-Minute Challenge* and check your answers.**

GRAMMAR

to be

1   Match sentences a–h with items 1–4. Write the letters in the boxes.

1   Bruno Mars   e
2   Maria Sharapova
3   sushi
4   cariocas

a   She's Russian.
b   It's Japanese.
c   They are Brazilian.
d   It's food.
e   He's a singer.
f   They are from Rio de Janeiro.
g   She's a tennis player.
h   He's American.

2   Look at the sentences from the radio quiz. Choose the correct words. Then complete the rule.

1   I *am* / *are* from London.
2   You *am* / *are* wrong.
3   They *am* / *are* from Rio de Janeiro in Brazil.

> **RULE:** The verb *to be* changes for different subject pronouns.
> I **am** American.
> You/We/They ¹_____ American.
> He/She/It ²_____ American.
> We often use contracted forms after pronouns.
> I am = I'm
> You/We/They are = You're / We're / They're
> He/She/It is = He's / She's / It's

LOOK!

Singular	Plural
I	we
you	you
he/she/it	they

3   Complete the sentences. Use contracted forms where possible.

0   I *'m* _____ from New York.
1   She _____ a famous actor.
2   Jacob _____ from the USA.
3   Liam and Ben _____ my best friends.
4   We _____ in Class 2B.
5   You _____ wrong. Sorry.

Workbook page 11 ➡

THiNK SELF-ESTEEM

The 'Me' flag

1   **Choose things that are important to you.**

● one colour
● one animal
● two activities

2   **SPEAKING** Use your ideas from Exercise 1 to draw your flag. Tell your partner about it.

My flag is blue and red. They're my favourite colours. Here is a football. It's my favourite sport. Here is music. I love music. Here is a panda. It's my favourite animal.

READING

1 🔊 1.21 **Read and listen to the dialogue. Who knows more about football, Jamie or Marta?**

JAMIE	Nice shirt.
MARTA	Thank you. It's the new Barcelona shirt.
JAMIE	I know. I'm a Barcelona fan, too. So what's your name?
MARTA	Marta. And what's your name?
JAMIE	I'm Jamie.
MARTA	Nice to meet you, Jamie.
JAMIE	Nice to meet you, too. Where are you from, Marta?
MARTA	I'm from Spain. I'm from a small town called Teruel.
JAMIE	Spain is a beautiful country.
MARTA	Yes, it is. So who's your favourite Barcelona player?
JAMIE	Umm … er … Tony Kroos?
MARTA	The German player?
JAMIE	Yes, he's great.
MARTA	Yes, he is. But he isn't a Barcelona player.
JAMIE	No?
MARTA	He's a Real Madrid player.
JAMIE	Oh!
MARTA	It's late. Time to go. Bye, Jamie.
JAMIE	Oh, OK!

2 **Read the dialogue again. Mark the sentences T (true) or F (false). Write the correct sentences.**

0 Jamie is a Real Madrid fan.　　　　　　　　 *F*
　Jamie is a Barcelona fan.
1 Marta is Spanish.
2 Marta is from a big town.
3 Tony Kroos is Italian.
4 Tony Kroos is a Barcelona player.

3 **Write the questions.**

1 Q _____
　A I'm Jamie.
2 Q _____
　A I'm from a small town called Teruel.
3 Q _____
　A Tony Kroos.

FUNCTIONS
Getting to know someone

1 🔊 1.22 **Put the dialogue in order. Listen and check.**

	GINA	Nice to meet you, too.
	GINA	I'm from Paris.
	GINA	Yes, it is.
	GINA	I'm Gina.
1	GINA	What's your name?
	PAOLO	Nice to meet you, Gina.
	PAOLO	Where are you from, Gina?
	PAOLO	Paris is a beautiful city.
	PAOLO	I'm Paolo. And you?

2 **SPEAKING** **Work in pairs. Act out the dialogue.**

3 **SPEAKING** **Work in pairs. Make your own dialogue.**

VOCABULARY
Adjectives

1 🔊 1.23 **Write the words in the list under the pictures. Listen and check.**

~~a big TV~~ | a dirty football | a fast car | a new pen
a slow bus | a small pizza | an expensive computer
an old phone | cheap tickets | clean shirts

0 _a big TV_

1 _____

2 _____

3 _____

4 _____

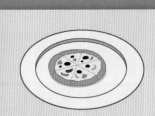

5 _____

7 _____

8 _____

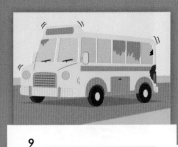

9 _____

6 _____

2 **Match the opposites.**

0	new	_d_	a	slow
1	big		b	expensive
2	dirty		c	small
3	cheap		d	old
4	fast		e	clean

3 **Put the words in order.**

0 old / computer / an
   an old computer

1 a / bike / new

2 expensive / an / restaurant

3 train / fast / a

4 dirty / shoes

5 book / cheap / a

> **LOOK!** In English, adjectives always stay the same.
> _new pens_ **NOT** ~~news pens~~
> _green cars_ **NOT** ~~greens cars~~

Workbook page 13 ➔

WRITING
Personal information

Look at the questionnaire. Answer the questions about you in full sentences.

The York English
Summer Camp

We're really excited about your visit next month. Answer the questions about yourself to find the perfect roommate.

What's your name?

_____

Where are you from?

_____

How old are you?

_____

Who's your favourite pop star?

_____

What's your favourite colour?

_____

Just a little joke

1 Look at the photos and answer the questions.

How many people can you see?
Where are they?

2 🔊 1.24 **Now read and listen to the photostory. Check your answers.**

RUBY Hi, Ellie.
ELLIE Hi, Ruby. How's it going?
RUBY Great, thanks. Oh, hello, Dan.
DAN Hi, you two.

1

RUBY Who's that?
DAN That's *Thomas.*
ELLIE Who's he?
DAN He's in my class. He's new.

2

ELLIE Where's he from?
DAN He's from Paris. He's cool. OK, time to go now. See you tomorrow.
RUBY Bye, Dan.
ELLIE See you later.

3

ELLIE He's from Paris?
RUBY Paris. That is so awesome!
ELLIE I know!

4

DEVELOPING SPEAKING

3 ▶ EP1 **Watch to find out how the story continues.**

1 Is Thomas from France?

2 Where is he from?

4 ▶ EP1 **Watch again. Choose the correct word in each sentence.**

0 They are in *an ice cream*/ *a fast food* shop.

1 The chocolate ice cream is for *Ellie* / *Ruby*.

2 Thomas (Tom) is *American* / *French*.

3 He's from *Paris, Texas* / *Paris, France*.

4 The ice cream *is very good* / *isn't very good*.

PHRASES FOR FLUENCY

1 Find the expressions 1–4 in the story. Who says them?

1 How's it going?

2 See you later.

3 That is so awesome!

4 I know!

2 How do you say the expressions in Exercise 1 in your language?

3 Change the underlined expressions. Use an expression from Exercise 1.

1 A This is my new bicycle.

  B Great!

2 Hi, George. How are you?

3 A This is a nice computer.

  B Yes, it is.

4 OK, I'm off now. Goodbye!

4 Complete the dialogues with the expressions from Exercise 1.

0 A Moscow is a city in Russia.

  B *I know* !

1 A Hello, Ben!

  B _____ ?

2 A Look at my new phone.

  B _____ !

3 A Goodbye, Mike.

  B _____ , Annie.

FUNCTIONS
Talking about yourself and others

1 Match the questions and answers.

0 Who's that? | *b*

1 Where's he from? |

2 How old are you? |

3 Who's your favourite singer? |

a He's from Paris.

b That's Thomas.

c Beyoncé.

d I'm 11.

2 Put the words in the correct order to make dialogues.

1 A that / who's ?
   Who's that?

  B Mary / that's .

  A she / from / where's ?

  B the UK / from / she's .

2 A they / are / who ?

  B Mario / are / and / they / Alex .

  A are / from / where / they ?

  B from / they / Mexico / are .

3 A Hi, / your / name / what's ?

  B Bob / I'm .

  A old / you, / how / are / Bob ?

  B 12 / I'm .

  A favourite / your / singer / who's ?

  B Ed Sheeran .

3 SPEAKING **Work in pairs. Act out the dialogues. Then make similar dialogues.**

2 I FEEL HAPPY

READING

1 Match the phrases with the photos. Write 1–6 in the boxes.

1	on a train	4	at school
2	on a plane	5	on a beach
3	at a stadium	6	on a bus

2 **SPEAKING** Work in pairs. Student A, close your book. Student B, test your partner.

> What's A?

> It's 'on a beach.'

3 ◀)) 1.25 Read and listen to the text messages on page 21. Where are the people? Write the names under the correct photos in Exercise 1.

4 Read the text messages again. Mark the sentences T (true) or F (false).

0	Nicky is worried.	T
1	Andrea is at school.	
2	Andrea, Amy and Katie are on holiday.	
3	Ryan is bored.	
4	The bus driver isn't angry.	
5	James isn't happy.	

A

B

C

D

E 1

F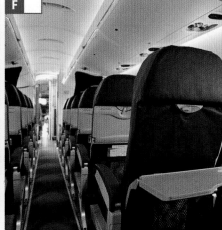

Hi there!

Nicky

Hi there, I'm at school. There are 12 girls and 15 boys in my new class. They aren't very friendly. I'm a little worried. 😟 But the teacher's really cool. How are you? Are you OK? See you soon.

10.06

Andrea

Look at my photo. I'm on the beach. It's hot and sunny. I'm very happy. 😌 I'm with 2 American girls, Amy and Katie. It's fun! What about you? How's your holiday? Is it nice there?

3.26

Ryan

I'm on the bus to school and I'm not very happy. It's so full and I'm very hot. 😡 The driver isn't very nice and he's angry. Ten more minutes to get to school. See you soon!

8.16

James

Hi, I'm at the stadium. It's 4–0 to the other team. The players in my team aren't good. Are they tired or bored? I'm sad. 🙁 Football is a great game, but this match isn't great. Bye.

4.58

▌THiNK VALUES ▌

Welcoming a new classmate

1 **Look at the picture and answer the questions.**

1 Where is Emily?
2 How is she?
3 Why isn't Emily happy?

The first day at my new school. I'm worried and I'm sad. Where are my friends?

2 **Imagine you are Emily's classmate. What's OK 🙂 or not OK 😟?**

0 talk to Emily   🙂
1 help Emily   _____
2 smile at Emily   _____
3 laugh at Emily   _____
4 not talk to Emily   _____
5 ask Emily questions   _____

3 **SPEAKING Compare your ideas with a partner.**

It's OK to smile at Emily.

It isn't OK to …

4 **SPEAKING Work in pairs. Think of other things you can do to help Emily on her first day.**

21

VOCABULARY
Adjectives to describe feelings

1 🔊 1.26 **Match the feelings in the list with the pictures. Write 1–10 in the boxes. Listen and check.**

1 angry | 2 bored | 3 cold | 4 excited
5 hot | 6 hungry | 7 sad | 8 thirsty
9 ~~tired~~ | 10 worried

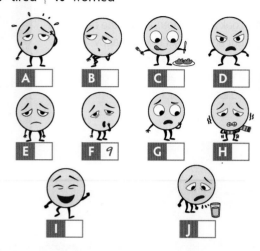

2 **Match the sentences with the pictures. Write 1–6 in the boxes.**

1 It's your birthday.
2 It's one o'clock in the morning.
3 There's a great film on TV but the TV is broken.
4 It's an awful day.
5 Your mum is angry with you.
6 You're on a plane.

3 **SPEAKING** Work in pairs. Tell your partner how you feel in the situations in Exercise 2. Your partner guesses the situation.

> I'm excited.

> Number 1?

Workbook page 21

GRAMMAR
to be (negative, singular and plural)

1 **Look at the text messages on page 21. Complete the sentences. Then complete the rule.**

1 They _____ very friendly.
2 The driver _____ very nice and he's angry.

> **RULE:** We form the negative of *to be* with subject + be + 1_____ .
> *I'm not* sad. (**am not**)
> *You aren't* sad. (**are not**)
> *He/She/It* 2_____ sad. (**is not**)
> *We aren't* sad. (**are not**)
> *They* 3_____ sad. (**are not**)

2 **Complete the sentences with the correct negative form of *to be*.**

0 Adelaide _*isn't*_ happy today. She's very sad.
1 You _____ in my team. You're in Mike's team.
2 They _____ eleven years old. They are ten.
3 No pizza for me, thanks. I _____ hungry.
4 Angie's favourite colour is blue. It _____ green.

3 **Complete the sentences with the correct form of *to be*.**

0 We __*'re*__ ✓ American. We __*aren't*__ ✗ British.
1 I _____ ✗ sad. I _____ ✓ happy!
2 Danny _____ ✓ twelve. He _____ ✗ eleven.
3 It _____ ✗ hot. It _____ ✓ cold!
4 Lucy _____ ✓ worried. She _____ ✗ excited.

Workbook page 18

> ## Pronunciation
> Vowel sounds – adjectives
> **Go to page 120.** 🔊

■ TRAIN TO THINK ■
Categorising

1 **Read the words in the list. Put them into four categories. There are four words for each category.**

afternoon | angry | book | bored | chair | desk
evening | excited | grey | morning | night
orange | pencil | purple | white | worried

2 **SPEAKING** Work in pairs. Compare your categories. Think of a title for each one.

> Category 1 - grey, orange, ...

LISTENING

1 ◀)) 1.29 **Listen to four dialogues. Match two of the dialogues with the pictures. Write a number (1–4) in the boxes.**

2 ◀)) 1.29 **Listen again. Complete the dialogues with *cold*, *tired*, *excited* and *angry*.**

0 **A** Is Noah's mum sad?

   B No, she isn't. She's ___angry___ .

1 **A** Are Chris and David worried?

   B No, they aren't. They're _____ .

2 **A** Is Ted worried?

   B No, he isn't. He's _____ .

3 **A** Is Ashley hot?

   B No, she isn't. She's very _____ .

GRAMMAR

to be (questions and short answers)

1 **Look at picture A in Exercise 1. Choose the correct answer. Then complete the rule and the table.**

A Are you hot, Ashley?

B *Yes, I am. / No, I'm not.*

> **RULE:** We form questions with [1]_____ + subject.
> We form short answers with [2]_____ + subject + *to be* (+ *not*).

Question	Short positive answer	Short negative answer
Am I in your team?	Yes, you **are**.	No, you **aren't**.
Are you OK?	Yes, I **am**.	No, I**'m** not.
[1]_____ he/she/it OK?	Yes, he/she/it **is**.	No, [4]_____ .
Are we in your team?	Yes, we are.	No, [5]_____ .
[2]_____ they OK?	Yes, they [3]_____ .	No, they **aren't**.

2 **Put the words in order to make questions. Write the answers.**

0 African / he / is / South / ? (yes)

   Is he South African? Yes, he is.

1 hungry / you / are / ? (no)

2 Brazil / they / from / are / ? (yes)

3 you / 12 / are / ? (yes)

4 she / is / tired / ? (no)

5 late / I / am / ? (no)

A ☐

B ☐

3 **Look at the rule again. Complete the dialogues.**

1 **A** _____*Are*_____ you angry, Keira?

   B No, I _____ . I'm just tired.

2 **A** _____ James and Tim your best friends?

   B Yes, they _____ . They _____ in my class at school.

3 **A** _____ Ms Brown your English teacher?

   B No, she _____ . She's my mother's friend.

4 **A** Am I in your team?

   B No, you _____ . You're in Pam's team.

5 **A** _____ Jules French?

   B _____ . He's from Paris.

6 **A** _____ we late?

   B _____ . We're early.

4 **SPEAKING** **Work in pairs. Ask and answer.**

> *Is football your favourite sport?*

> *Are you cold?*

> *Are your best friends from the USA?*

> *Is your teacher in the classroom?*

5 **SPEAKING** **Think of three more questions to ask your partner. Then ask and answer.**

Workbook page 18 ▶

READING

1 🔊 1.30 **Read and listen to the dialogue and choose the correct option.**

Nick and Connor decide to …
a go to the cinema. ☐
b listen to music. ☐
c go to a club for young people. ☐

2 **Read the dialogue again. Number the photos in the order that Connor talks about them. Write 1–5 in the boxes.**

CONNOR	What's the matter, Nick? Are you tired?
NICK	Tired? No, no. I'm not tired. I'm bored.
CONNOR	Why are you bored?
NICK	Because there's nothing to do. Nothing to do at all.
CONNOR	Well, there's a Formula One race at five. It's on TV.
NICK	Formula One? I don't like it.
CONNOR	Really? What about a film? There's a new film on at the cinema.
NICK	A film? Who's in it?
CONNOR	Ben Stiller. He's so funny.
NICK	Ben Stiller? I don't like him. He's not funny. He's terrible.
CONNOR	Erm. What about some music? Listen to this song. It's the new one from One Direction.
NICK	One Direction! Are you joking? I don't like them.
CONNOR	Well do you like ice cream? The new ice cream shop in town is open.
NICK	Ice cream? No, I don't like it.
CONNOR	What! You don't like ice cream?
NICK	No, I don't.
CONNOR	OK, what about the club?
NICK	What club?
CONNOR	The new club for teenagers.
NICK	Hmm, I'm not sure.
CONNOR	But Jenny is a member.
NICK	Jenny?
CONNOR	Yes, Jenny Carter.
NICK	Jenny Carter?
CONNOR	Yes, she goes there every Friday.
NICK	Really? Let's go!

3 **Correct the sentences.**

0 Nick is tired.
He isn't tired. He's bored.
1 The Formula One race is at eight.
2 Johnny Depp is in the film.
3 The song is by The Feeling.
4 The new T-shirt shop in town is open.
5 Nick is a member of the club for teenagers.

A ☐

B ☐

C ☐

D ☐ 1

E ☐

GRAMMAR
Object pronouns

1 Complete the dialogues with *them*, *it* and *him*. Read the dialogue on page 24 again and check. Then use the words to complete the table.

CONNOR	There's a Formula One race at five.
NICK	Formula One? I don't like [1]_____ .
CONNOR	Ben Stiller is so funny.
NICK	I don't like [2]_____ .
CONNOR	Listen to this song.
NICK	One Direction! I don't like [3]_____ .

Subject	Object
I	me
you	you
he	[1]_____
she	her
it	[2]_____
we	us
they	[3]_____

2 Complete the dialogues with the correct object pronouns.

0 A Dad's angry.
   B Yes, he isn't very happy with ___us___ , Tom.
1 A Do you like Maroon 5?
   B No, I don't like _____ .
2 A Do you like Jennifer Lopez?
   B Yes, I like _____ . She's great.
3 A Do you like _____ ?
   B Yes, I think you and Peter are great.
4 A Do you like _____ ?
   B Yes, I think Jack is funny.
5 A Do you like my new bike?
   B Yes, I like _____ .
6 A Bob, I really like _____ .
   B I really like you too, Alice.

Workbook page 19

VOCABULARY
Positive and negative adjectives

1 Look at the words in the list. Write N (negative) or P (positive) in the boxes.

awful [N] | bad [ ] | excellent [P] | exciting [ ]
funny [ ] | good [ ] | great [ ] | terrible [ ]

2 **SPEAKING** Work in pairs. Give one example for each of the following.

> *How To Train Your Dragon 2 is a funny film.*

a a funny film
b an excellent actor
c a bad film
d an exciting computer game
e a great sportsperson
f a terrible singer
g a great country
h a good book
i an awful actor

Workbook page 21

FUNCTIONS
Expressing likes and dislikes

1 Which of these sentences means 'is good'? Which means 'is bad'?

1 I don't like Taylor Swift.
2 I like Shakira.

2 Put the words in the correct order to make questions.

A you / like / The Rolling Stones / do / ?
B you / Katy Perry / like / do / ?

3 Match the answers to the questions in Exercise 2.

1 No, I don't like them. They're terrible. [ ]
2 Yes, I like her. She's great. [ ]

4 **SPEAKING** Work in pairs. Talk about the films, actors, bands or singers you really like / don't like.

> *Do you like Lorde?*

> *Yes, I like her. I think she's great.*

> *Do you like the Divergent films?*

> *No, I don't like them. They're terrible.*

Masks from around the world

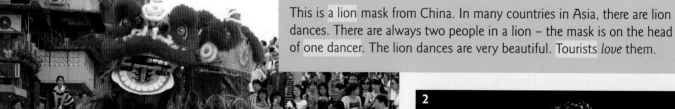

This is a lion mask from China. In many countries in Asia, there are lion dances. There are always two people in a lion – the mask is on the head of one dancer. The lion dances are very beautiful. Tourists *love* them.

The masks here are from Greece. They are 2,000 years old. They are masks for the actors in the Greek theatre.

This mask is from North America. It's a mask from the First Nations people in Canada. The mask is for the medicine man.

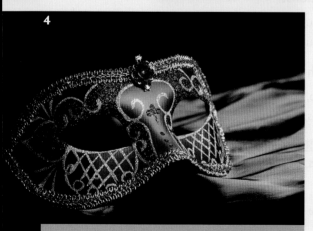

Masks are an important part of the carnival in Venice, Italy. There are many different types of carnival masks. For example, the mask in this picture is called the Colombina. Carnival masks are often very beautiful and some are very expensive.

These are Halloween masks. Halloween is on 31st October. Children in many countries around the world, for example, the USA and the UK, wear Halloween masks. They go from house to house and say 'Trick or treat'. People give them sweets ('treats').

1 Look at the photos on page 26. Find these things.

masks | a lion
a mask from the First Nations people
one dancer | sweets | tourists

2 What feelings can you see in the masks?

> *Mask number 1 is happy.*

3 🔊 1.31 Read and listen to the article. Which countries are the masks from?

4 Read the article again. Mark the sentences T (true) or F (false).

0 The Lion dance is from Canada.   **F**

1 The North American mask is for a doctor.

2 The Greek masks are 200 years old.

3 Halloween is only a holiday in the USA and the UK.

4 Colombina is a type of Italian mask.

5 **SPEAKING** Which of the masks do you like? Which do you not like? Why? Tell your partner.

WRITING
Describing feelings and things

1 Read the text messages. Write the names under the photos.

2 Read the text messages again and answer the questions.

1 Where is Henry?
2 Is he happy?
3 Why? / Why not?
4 Where is Tom?
5 Is he happy?
6 Why? / Why not?

3 How do Tom and Henry …

1 start their text?
2 finish their text?

4 Imagine you want to write a text message to a friend. Think of answers to these questions.

1 Where are you?
2 Are you happy?
3 Why? / Why not?

5 Use your answers in Exercise 4 to write a text message (35–50 words) to a friend.

> **Tom**
>
> Hi, Sara. I'm at school. It's lunchtime and I'm really hungry. But I'm sad. The lunch at school today isn't good. I'm also cold. The sun isn't out. It's not a great day. What about you? Is your day good? Bye.
>
> *21/1, 13.12*

> **Henry**
>
> Hi, Annie. I'm in the car with my family. I'm excited because I'm on holiday. Yeah! Two more hours to get to the beach! How are you? Are you OK? See you soon!
>
> *16/6, 10.03*

A _____

B _____

■ THiNK EXAMS ■

READING AND WRITING
Part 3: Multiple-choice replies

1 **Complete the five conversations. Choose the correct answer A, B or C.**

0	What's your name?	A	I'm 11.
		Ⓑ	It's Kylie.
		C	Yes, I am.

1	How old are you?	A	I'm Brazilian.
		B	I'm 12.
		C	It's John.

2	Are we late?	A	Yes, we are.
		B	No, I'm not.
		C	Yes, he is.

3	Do you like Beyoncé?	A	No, I like her.
		B	Yes, I am.
		C	Yes, I like her.

4	Where are you from?	A	I'm 13.
		B	Yes, I am.
		C	Mexico.

5	Is Tom your friend?	A	Yes, we are.
		B	Yes, he is.
		C	Yes, I am.

Part 2: Multiple-choice sentence completion

2 **Read the sentences about Jim. Choose the best word (A, B or C) for each space.**

0 Hi, my name _____ Jim.

A am   Ⓑ is   C are

1 It _____ my birthday today.

A are   B am   C is

2 I _____ 12 years old.

A am   B is   C are

3 I am _____ my school.

A at   B on   C to

4 I like Ed Sheeran. He's a(n) _____ singer.

A great   B awful   C terrible

5 I _____ like sport.

A aren't   B don't   C isn't

TEST YOURSELF

VOCABULARY

1 **Complete the sentences with the words in the list. There are two extra words.**

awful | Brazil | clean | excited | expensive | hot
hungry | old | Russian | Spain | Spanish | thirsty

1 I want a sandwich. I'm _____ .
2 She's from Moscow. She's _____ .
3 Open the window, please. I'm _____ !
4 This pizza is _____ . I don't like it!
5 He's _____ . I think he's from Madrid.
6 I'm 12 and my big brother Jack is 23. He's _____ !
7 Are you _____ ? OK, here's a glass of water.
8 £175? Oh, it's very _____ .
9 Brasilia is a big city in _____ .
10 We're on the train to Paris! We're very _____ !

/10

GRAMMAR

2 **Complete the sentences with the words in the list.**

don't | her | How | it | Where | Why

1 Mike and Annie aren't here. _____ are they?
2 This is my new shirt. I really like _____ .
3 She's my friend. I like _____ a lot.
4 _____ old are you?
5 I _____ like hamburgers.
6 A _____ are you here?
  B Because it's a nice place.

3 **Find and correct the mistake in each sentence.**

1 I not like football.
2 What old is your brother?
3 Are them from Italy?
4 It aren't an expensive computer.
5 He's the new boy in the class. I like he.
6 What is your favourite singer?

/12

FUNCTIONAL LANGUAGE

4 **Write the missing words.**

1 A Who _____ she?
  B She's Maria. She's _____ Mexico.
2 A _____ are they from?
  B Spain. They _____ Spanish.
3 A _____ you like Taylor Swift?
  B Yes, I do. She _____ a great singer.
4 A I _____ like this film. It's awful!
  B Oh, really? I _____ it. It's funny!

/8

MY SCORE /30

| 22 – 30 |
| 10 – 21 |
| 0 – 9 |

3 | ME AND MY FAMILY

A

B

C

D 1

READING

1 Match the family members with the photos. Write 1–4 in the boxes.

1 brother and sister
2 mother and son
3 father and daughter
4 husband and wife

2 SPEAKING Think of famous examples of the following. Tell your partner.

1 a husband and wife
2 a mother and daughter
3 a father and son
4 sisters
5 brothers

> Brad Pitt and Angelina Jolie are a famous husband and wife.

3 SPEAKING Look at the photos on page 31. Use words from Exercise 1 to talk about the people.

4 ◀)) 1.32 Read and listen to the article. Mark the sentences T (true) or F (false).

0	Kate Middleton is from England.	T
1	She's got three brothers and sisters.	
2	Kate's picture is never in the newspapers.	
3	William's father is Prince Charles.	
4	Kate's home is new.	
5	Kate and William's apartment is small.	

Kate Middleton

Kate Middleton is an English woman. She likes sport (especially hockey) and photography. She's a very busy person. She works with many organisations to help children and sportspeople.

Kate's family is from Berkshire in England. She has a sister called Pippa and a brother called James.

So, is she a normal woman?

Not really. Now, she's famous all over the world. Her photograph is often in the newspapers and she's often on TV. She's The Duchess of Cambridge. Her husband is Prince William, the Duke of Cambridge. William's father is Prince Charles and his grandmother is Queen Elizabeth II of Britain.

William and Kate have a son called George and a daughter called Charlotte. George was born in 2013 and Charlotte was born in 2015.

Kate and William's home is an apartment in Kensington Palace, in London. The palace is 300 years old. Their apartment is really big, with twenty bedrooms and three kitchens.

■ THiNK VALUES ■

Families

1 **Complete the sentences with at least one word from the list. Use a dictionary to help you.**

friendly | interested in … | patient
helpful | kind | strict | generous

1 A good brother/sister is _____ .
2 A good father is _____ .
3 A good mother is _____ .
4 A good grandfather/grandmother is _____ .

2 **SPEAKING** **Compare your ideas with others in the class.**

GRAMMAR
Possessive 's

1 **Look at the examples. Then complete the rule.**

1 Kate's family is from Berkshire in England.
2 William's father is Prince Charles.

> **RULE:** We talk about possession with noun + 's.
> Peter _____ sister = the sister of Peter

2 **Look at the photos and write the correct words with 's.**

my sister

0 _____my sister's phone_____

Patrick

1 _____

Mrs White

2 _____

my cousin

3 _____

Wendy

4 _____

my uncle

5 _____

> **LOOK!** We use **'s** for both possessives and contractions.
> Tom**'s** house is big. (~~The house of Tom is big.~~)
> She**'s** my cousin. (She is my cousin.)

Workbook page 28

VOCABULARY
Family members

1 🔊 **1.33** **Complete Nicolás' family tree with the words in the list. Then listen and check.**

aunt | brother | cousin | father | grandfather | ~~grandmother~~ | mother | sister | uncle

Maria — 0 _grandmother_
José — 1 _____

Pablo — 2 _____
Susana — 3 _____
Jaime — 4 _____
Marta — 5 _____

Nicolás — 6 _____
Antonio — 7 _____
Ana —
Sara — 8 _____

2 **Look at the text on page 31. Complete the sentences with the words in the list.**

brother | ~~father~~ | grandfather | son | wife

0 William is George's ___*father*___ .
1 Kate is William's _____ .
2 George is Kate's _____ .
3 Prince Charles is George's _____ .
4 James is Kate and Pippa's _____ .

3 **SPEAKING** **Write three or four sentences about your family. Tell your partner.**

> My uncle Antonio is my mother's brother.

Workbook page 31

GRAMMAR
Possessive adjectives

1 Look at the article on page 31. Complete the sentences and match them with the people. Then complete the table.

1 _____ grandmother is Queen Elizabeth. ☐

2 _____ husband is Prince William. ☐

3 _____ apartment is really big. ☐

a William and Kate

b William

c Kate

Subject	Possessive adjective
I	my
you	your
he	1 _____
she	2 _____
it	its
we	our
they	3 _____

2 Complete the dialogue with words from Exercise 1.

STEVE Hello. ⁰ _My_ name's Steve. What's ¹_____ name?

JANE Hi. I'm Jane and this is Renata. She's Brazilian. She's here on holiday with ²_____ mother and father.

STEVE Hi, Renata.

RENATA Hi, Steve. How are you?

STEVE Fine, thanks. So, you and ³_____ parents are from Brazil?

RENATA That's right – we speak Portuguese. It's ⁴_____ first language.

JANE Have you got any brothers or sisters?

RENATA No, just me! And you?

JANE Yes, I've got two brothers. ⁵_____ names are Alex and Ricky. They love football! And they love Brazilian football!

RENATA Great! My father is a football fan, too – ⁶_____ favourite team is Flamengo.

Workbook page 28 ➤

LISTENING

1 🔊 1.34 Listen to three people talking about their family. Write 1–3 in the boxes.

2 🔊 1.34 Listen again and complete the sentences. Write one word in each space.

1 Jordan's family is very _____ . His uncle Jack is always very _____ .

2 Tania's _____ are in Australia. Her _____ Clare is nice but sometimes she's difficult, too.

3 Manuel has _____ cousins. His cousin Monica is very _____ to her brothers, sisters and friends.

■ THiNK SELF-ESTEEM ■
Being part of a family

1 Complete the 'ME' table. Write the names of four people in your family who are important to you and a word to describe them.

ME

	Name	Adjective
1		
2		
3		
4		

PARTNER

	Name	Adjective
1		
2		
3		
4		

2 **SPEAKING** Work in pairs. Ask your partner what he/she wrote. Write his/her answers in the 'PARTNER' table.

3 **SPEAKING** Tell the class about …

a your table.

b your partner's table.

READING

1 🔊 1.35 **Read and listen to the dialogue and answer the questions.**

   1 Where are the two girls?

   2 Who is Brian?

2 **Read the dialogue again and answer the questions.**

   1 Who's in the photograph?

   2 Does Agata like her brother Brian?

   3 Are the books and magazines Brian's?

   4 Are the DVDs Agata's?

   5 Does Brian like his sister?

AGATA	So, ⁰ *this* is my bedroom. Do you like it?
DEBBIE	Yes! It's really nice. I like your bed. And the curtains are great!
AGATA	Thank you. I like my room, too. It's my favourite room in the house – of course!
DEBBIE	¹_____ is a nice photograph. There, on the desk.
AGATA	Yes, it's me and my family, on holiday in Ibiza. We're all very happy in that photograph!
DEBBIE	Cool. And is ²_____ your brother?
AGATA	Yes, it is. ³_____ is Brian.
DEBBIE	Oh, he's nice.
AGATA	Hmm … sometimes he is, sometimes he isn't.
BRIAN	Agata! Are you in here?
AGATA	Hi, Brian. Yes, I'm here. And ⁴_____ is my friend Debbie.
BRIAN	Hello, Debbie. Listen, Agata – are ⁵_____ your things?
AGATA	What things?
BRIAN	The books and magazines.
AGATA	Oh, yes, sorry.
BRIAN	And Agata, the DVDs on your bed – ⁶_____ are my DVDs!
AGATA	Yes, you're right. Sorry again.
BRIAN	You know something, Debbie? Sometimes my sister isn't my favourite person!

3 🔊 1.35 **Complete the dialogue with the words in the list. Listen and check.**

this (x2) | that (x3) | these | those

GRAMMAR

this / that / these / those

1 **Match the sentences with the pictures. Write 1–4 in the boxes. Then choose the correct words to complete the rule.**

A ☐

B 1

C ☐

D ☐

   1 This is my sister.

   2 That's my brother.

   3 These are my pens.

   4 Those are my friends.

> **RULE:** The words **this** and **that** are ¹*singular / plural*.
>
> The words **these** and **those** are ²*singular / plural*.
>
> We use **this** and **these** to talk about things that are ³*near to / far from* us.
>
> We use **that** and **those** to talk about things that are ⁴*near to / far from* us.

2 **Look at the pictures in Exercise 1 again. Complete the sentences with *this, that, these* or *those*.**

   0 **Picture A:** Is _*this*_ your phone?

   1 **Picture B:** Are _____ your books?

   2 **Picture C:** Are _____ your books?

   3 **Picture D:** Is _____ your phone?

Workbook page 29 ➤

Pronunciation

this / that / these / those

Go to page 120. 🔊

VOCABULARY
House and furniture

1 🔊1.38 **Match the rooms in the picture with the words. Write 1–7 in the boxes. Listen and check.**

bathroom	
bedroom	
garage	1
garden	
hall	
kitchen	
living room	

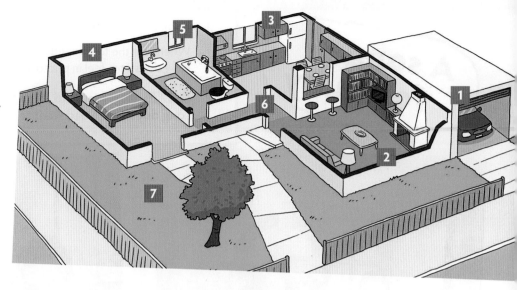

2 🔊1.39 **Match the words with the photos. Write 1–8 in the boxes. Listen and check.**

1 armchair | **2** bath | **3** bed | **4** cooker | **5** fridge | **6** shower | **7** sofa | **8** toilet

A [ ]   B [ ]   C [ ]   D [ ]

E [ ]   F [ ]   G [1]   H [ ]

3 **Complete the table with words A–H from Exercise 2.**

Living room	Kitchen	Bedroom	Bathroom

4 **SPEAKING** **Draw an unusual house. Put the furniture in different rooms. Tell your partner about your house.**

> The fridge is in the living room.
> The toilet is in the kitchen.

Workbook page 31

WRITING
Your favourite room

1 **Think about your favourite room in your house. Answer the questions.**

- Which room is it?
- Is it big or small?
- What things are in the room?
- What colours are the things in the room?

2 **Write a description of your favourite room (about 50 words).**

A song for Ruby

1 Look at the photos and answer the questions.

Where are the four friends?
How does Tom feel in photo 4?

2 ◀)) 1.40 Now read and listen to the photostory. What song does Tom's dad want to play?

TOM Come in, guys.
RUBY Wow, this photo is cool!
TOM Thank you.
DAN What's that photo over there?

1

TOM That's my family. We're on holiday.
RUBY It looks great. So, these are your parents and …
ELLIE … that's your sister?
TOM No, that's my cousin. My sister is there.
ELLIE Oh, right. She looks like your sister!

2

DAD Hello, everyone.
DAN Hello.
TOM Dad, these are my friends. This is Dan, and that's Ellie, and this is Ruby.

3

DAD Ruby? Really?
RUBY Yes. Why?
DAD Well, there's a great song called *Ruby*. Just a minute. Where's my guitar?
TOM OK, guys, let's go. I want to show you my room.

4

DEVELOPING SPEAKING

3 ▶**EP2** Watch to find out how the story continues.

1 What things do Tom's friends like about the house?

2 Do they like Tom's dad?

4 ▶**EP2** Watch again. Match the parts of the sentences.

0	Tom isn't very happy	*f*
1	Tom isn't a big fan of car racing,	
2	The armchair in Tom's room	
3	The garden in Tom's house	
4	They listen to music	
5	Ruby says Tom's dad	

a is broken.

b is really cool.

c in the living room.

d but he likes the poster of a racing car.

e isn't very big.

f about his dad.

PHRASES FOR FLUENCY

1 Find the expressions 1–4 in the story. Who says them?

1 Let's go.

2 Oh, right.

3 Really?

4 Just a minute.

2 How do you say the expressions in Exercise 1 in your language?

3 Put the sentences in the correct order to make a dialogue.

	TOM	Just a minute. Let me look at the map.
	TOM	Thanks. Oh. Sorry, Sally, this is the wrong map.
	TOM	Thanks. Ah, we're on the right road. Let's go.
1	SALLY	Where are we?
	SALLY	Really? Oh, right. Sorry. Here's the right map.
	SALLY	OK. The map's here. Here you are.

4 Complete the dialogues with the expressions from Exercise 1.

1 A I love this band. They're fantastic.

B _____ ? I don't like them.

2 A This is a photo of my best friend.

B _____ . She's very nice.

3 A Are you ready?

B _____ , where's my phone?

Oh, here it is. _____ .

FUNCTIONS
Paying compliments

1 Read the phrases. Tick (✓) five compliments.

1	This photo looks cool.	✓
2	Thank you.	
3	That's nice!	
4	That's my family.	
5	That's great.	
6	What a nice (picture)!	
7	I really like (your music).	

2 Tick the situations when you pay a compliment.

1	Your friend has got a new shirt.
2	It's a sunny day.
3	Your friend's sister is in New York on holiday.
4	There is a great poster on your friend's bedroom wall.
5	It's your friend's birthday.
6	You like your friend's cat.

3 Put the sentences in the correct order to make dialogues.

1 | *1* | A This photo is great.
   | | A Is that your sister in the photo? She looks nice.
   | | B Yes, her name's Carol. She's 14.
   | | B Thanks. I like it, too.

2 | | A Where's it from?
   | | A I really like your shirt.
   | | B Oh, thank you.
   | | B It's from my holiday in Brazil.

4 **SPEAKING** Act out the dialogues. Then change them and make similar dialogues.

4 IN THE CITY

OBJECTIVES

FUNCTIONS: talking about places in a town/city; giving directions; buying in a shop

GRAMMAR: *there is / there are*; *some / any*; imperatives

VOCABULARY: places in a town/city; prepositions of place; numbers 100+; prices

READING

1 **Match the phrases in the list with the photos. Write 1–4 in the boxes.**

1 a famous square | 2 a famous tower
3 a famous palace | 4 a famous statue

2 **SPEAKING** **Work in pairs. Can you name the places in the photographs? Where are they?**

> *I think it's the Eiffel Tower. It's in Paris.*

3 **◀) 1.41** **Read and listen to the brochure. Which two things in Exercise 1 are in *Window of the World*?**

4 **Read the brochure again. Mark the sentences T (true) or F (false).**

0 *Window of the World* is in China.   **T**

1 All the models are of things in the same country.

2 There are models of 130 different things.

3 You can ski at *Window of the World*.

4 There is a train station in the park.

5 There are restaurants at *Window of the World*.

5 **SPEAKING** **Work in pairs. Ask and answer the questions.**

1 Would you like to go to *Window of the World*?

2 What would you like to see there?

A

B

C

D 1

Window of the World

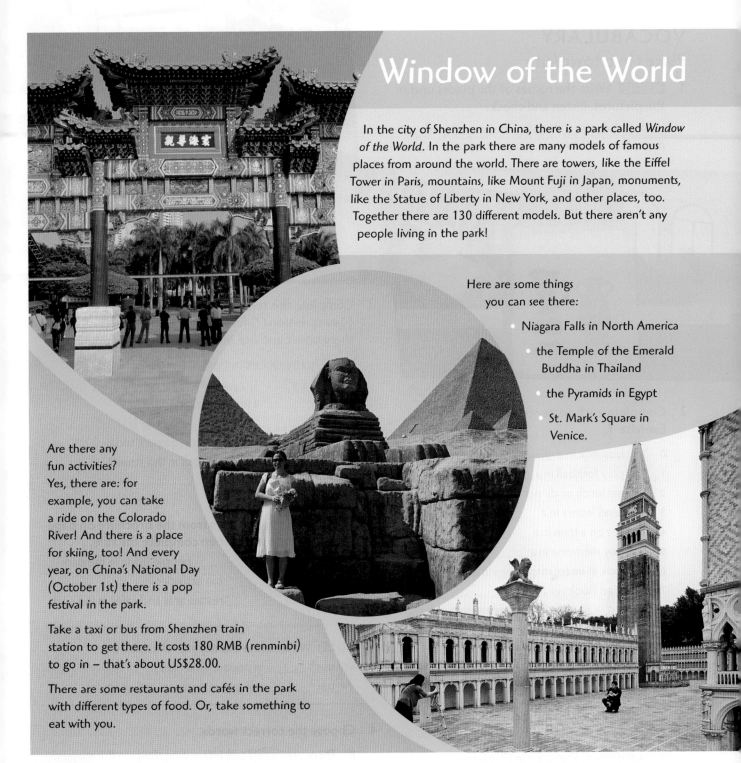

In the city of Shenzhen in China, there is a park called *Window of the World*. In the park there are many models of famous places from around the world. There are towers, like the Eiffel Tower in Paris, mountains, like Mount Fuji in Japan, monuments, like the Statue of Liberty in New York, and other places, too. Together there are 130 different models. But there aren't any people living in the park!

Here are some things you can see there:

- Niagara Falls in North America
- the Temple of the Emerald Buddha in Thailand
- the Pyramids in Egypt
- St. Mark's Square in Venice.

Are there any fun activities? Yes, there are: for example, you can take a ride on the Colorado River! And there is a place for skiing, too! And every year, on China's National Day (October 1st) there is a pop festival in the park.

Take a taxi or bus from Shenzhen train station to get there. It costs 180 RMB (renminbi) to go in – that's about US$28.00.

There are some restaurants and cafés in the park with different types of food. Or, take something to eat with you.

THiNK VALUES

My town/city

1 Think of your town/city and answer the questions.

  1 What are the most interesting places for you?
  2 What are the most interesting places for a visitor?

2 **SPEAKING** Make one list of interesting places for you and one for a visitor. Tell your partner.

  > The most interesting places in my town/city for me are …

  > The most interesting places in my town/city for a visitor are …

3 Think of a place in your town, city or country to put in *Window of the World*.

  1 What's the name of the place?
  2 Why do you want it in *Window of the World*?

  > I want to put … from my city because it's very old and beautiful.

4 **SPEAKING** Compare your ideas with others in the class.

VOCABULARY
Places in a town/city

1 🔊 1.42 **Write the names of the places under the pictures. Listen and check.**

bank | chemist's | library | museum | ~~park~~
post office | restaurant | supermarket | train station

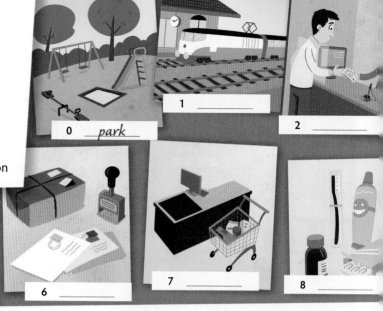

0 _park_

1 _____

2 _____

3 _____

4 _____

5 _____

6 _____

7 _____

8 _____

2 **Complete each sentence with a place from Exercise 1.**

0 You buy milk in a _supermarket_ .

1 You play football in a _____ .

2 You eat lunch or dinner in a _____ .

3 You send letters in a _____ .

4 You get on a train in a _____ .

5 You buy medicine in a _____ .

6 You look at interesting things in a _____ .

7 You read books in a _____ .

Workbook page 39

GRAMMAR
there is / there are

1 **Complete the sentences from the brochure on page 39. Use *is*, *are* and *aren't*. Then complete the table.**

1 In the city of Shenzhen in China, there _____ a park called *Window of the World*.

2 _____ there any fun activities?

3 But there _____ any people living in the park!

	Singular nouns	Plural nouns
Positive	There 1_____	There 3_____
Negative	There isn't	There 4_____
Questions	2_____ there?	5_____ there?

2 **Complete the sentences in the positive (+), negative (-) or question (?) form. Use *there is*, *there are*, *is there*, *there aren't* and *are there*.**

0 _There are_ six bridges in the city. (+)

1 _____ any good films on TV tonight. (-)

2 _____ a museum in your town?

3 _____ a great café near here. (+)

4 _____ any people in the park today. (-)

5 _____ any nice shops in this street?

some / any

3 **Complete the sentences from the brochure on page 39 with *some* or *any*. Then complete the rule.**

1 But there aren't _____ people living in the park!

2 Are there _____ fun activities?

3 There are _____ restaurants and cafés in the park.

> **RULE:** We use **some** and **any** with plural nouns.
> We use 1_____ in positive sentences.
> We use 2_____ in negative sentences and questions.

4 **Choose the correct words.**

0 There are (some) / any interesting things in the museum.

1 There aren't *some* / *any* parks in my town.

2 Are there *some* / *any* good shops here?

3 There are *some* / *any* nice places to eat here.

5 **SPEAKING** **Work in pairs. Think of a city, but don't tell your partner! Ask and answer questions to find out the cities.**

Is there a famous park in your city? *Yes, there is.*

Is there a famous statue? *Yes, there is.*

Is it New York?

Workbook page 36

VOCABULARY
Prepositions of place

1 Look at the map and complete the sentences with the words in the list.

behind | between | in front of | next to
~~on the corner (of)~~ | opposite

1 A is _on the corner (of)_ Green Street and High Street and _____ the supermarket.
2 B is _____ the library.
3 C is _____ the bank.
4 D is _____ the park and the post office.
5 E is _____ the restaurant.

Workbook page 39 ▶

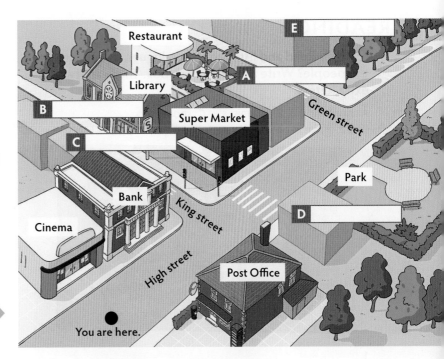

Restaurant
Library
Super Market
Green street
Park
Bank
King street
Cinema
Post Office
High street
E
A
B
C
D
You are here.

LISTENING

1 🔊 1.43 Listen to three people asking for directions. Write *museum*, *chemist's* and *shopping centre* in the correct places on the map. There are two extra spaces.

2 🔊 1.43 Listen again and complete the sentences.

0 The chemist's is _____opposite_____ the library.
1 The chemist's is _____ the bank.
2 The museum is on _____ Green Street.
3 The shopping centre is _____ a restaurant.

2 Match the parts of the sentences.

0 Listen ... [b]
1 Sit
2 Don't open
3 Don't look
4 Turn
5 Go

a the door.
b to me.
c right.
d down, please.
e down the street.
f at the answers.

Workbook page 37 ▶

GRAMMAR
Imperatives

1 Complete the examples with *don't*, *turn* and *go*. Then complete the rule.

1 _____ past the supermarket.
2 _____ left.
3 _____ take a bus – it's only two minutes from here.

RULE: To tell someone to do something, you can use the **imperative** – it's the same as the base form of the verb.

To tell someone **not** to do something, use
[1] _____ + the base form of the verb.

FUNCTIONS
Giving directions

1 **SPEAKING** Work in pairs. Look at the map again. Student A: You're at the restaurant. Student B: Think of another place on the map, but don't say it! Tell Student A how to find you.

OK, turn right and right again into High Street. Turn right into King Street. It's on the right.

The supermarket?

That's right!

2 **SPEAKING** Now change. Student B: You're in the park. Student A: Choose another place on the map and tell Student B how to get there.

READING

1 🔊 1.44 **Read and listen to the dialogues. Where are the people? Write a letter in each box. There are two extra letters.**

A bookshop | B chemist's | C shoe shop
D supermarket | E train station

1 ☐

MAN	Morning. Can I ^{0} *help you* ?
GIRL	Yes, please. A ticket to London, please.
MAN	Return?
GIRL	Yes, please – a day return. ^{1}_____ is it?
MAN	Well, it's £27.50 – but you can't come back between four o'clock and seven o'clock.
GIRL	Oh, no problem. Here you are – thirty pounds.
MAN	Thank you. And … two pounds fifty change.
GIRL	Thanks a lot.
MAN	OK. Oh! Don't forget your tickets!
GIRL	Oh, yes – thanks. Silly me.

2 ☐

WOMAN	These are nice. I really like them.
MAN	Yes, they're really nice.
WOMAN	And they're very comfortable. How much ^{2}_____ ?
MAN	They're £120.
WOMAN	Wow. They're expensive.
MAN	Yes, but they're beautiful shoes.
WOMAN	You're right. OK, I'll ^{3}_____ them.
MAN	Great!

3 ☐

WOMAN	Hello.
GIRL	Hi. ^{4}_____ take these, please?
WOMAN	OK. Wow, that's a lot of books.
GIRL	That's right. There are twelve. Well, I'm a student.
WOMAN	Oh, right! So, here we go. Right – that's £135, please.
GIRL	OK. Here's my credit card.
WOMAN	Thank you. OK, bye – have ^{5}_____ .
GIRL	You too. Thank you!

2 **Complete the dialogues with the words and phrases in the list.**

a nice day | are they | Can I
~~help you~~ | How much | take

3 **SPEAKING** **Work in pairs. Act out the dialogues.**

VOCABULARY
Numbers 100+

1 🔊 1.45 **Match the words with the numbers. Then listen, check and repeat.**

0	130	d
1	150	
2	175	
3	200	
4	560	
5	1,000	
6	1,200	
7	2,000	

a five hundred and sixty
b one thousand two hundred
c two hundred
d one hundred and thirty
e one hundred and seventy-five
f one thousand
g two thousand
h one hundred and fifty

> **LOOK!** When a number is more than 100, we use the word **and**:
>
> one hundred **and** twenty
> two hundred **and** sixty-five
>
> We **don't** use the word and for numbers 20–99.
>
> twenty-five **NOT** ~~twenty and five~~
> seventy-three **NOT** ~~seventy and three~~

2 🔊 1.46 **Listen and write the numbers.**

Workbook page 39

> **Pronunciation**
> **Word stress in numbers**
> **Go to page 120.** 🔊

VOCABULARY
Prices

1 🔊 1.49 **Say these prices. Listen and check.**

1 £15.00
2 $25.00
3 €230.00
4 £9.99
5 $21.95
6 €72.50

> **LOOK!** $ = dollar(s)   £ = pound(s)   € = euro(s)
> £2.50 – In everyday English, we say *two pounds fifty* **not** *two pounds and fifty pence*.

2 🔊 1.50 **Listen and look at the prices. Number them in the order you hear them.**

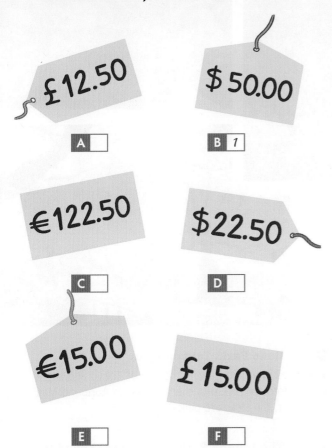

£12.50 **A** ☐	$50.00 **B** 1
€122.50 **C** ☐	$22.50 **D** ☐
€15.00 **E** ☐	£15.00 **F** ☐

3 **SPEAKING** Work in pairs. Ask and answer the questions. Student A: Go to page 127. Student B: Go to page 128.

Workbook page 39 ➡

FUNCTIONS
Buying in a shop

1 **Read these questions and answers. Who says them? Write C (customer) or A (shop assistant).**

1 Can I help you? — *A*
2 I'll take them. ☐
3 How much are they? ☐
4 Here's your change. ☐
5 That's £ … , please. ☐
6 Have you got … ? ☐

2 **Use the questions and answers from Exercise 1 to complete the dialogue. Write 1–6.**

A Hi there. ___1___
B Hello. Yes, please. _____ any music magazines?
A Sure. There's this one here and there's also this one.
B Great. _____
A This one is £3.95 and the other one is £3.50.
B OK – _____
A Great. _____ £7.45, _____
B OK, Here you are. £10.00.
A Thank you. _____ – £2.55.
B Thanks. Bye!

3 🔊 1.51 **Listen and check. Then act out the dialogue with a partner.**

■ TRAIN TO THiNK ■
Exploring numbers

1 **Read, think and write the answers.**

> Susan, Ian and George go shopping. Susan has got £20. Ian has got £12 and George has got £2. Susan spends £1.40 at the book shop and £3.30 at the supermarket and £8.30 at the café. Ian spends £3.80 at the post office and £2.20 at the chemist's.

At home, Mum says, 'How much money have you got now?'

Susan: £_____
Ian: £_____
George: £_____

2 **Then Mum says: 'OK, Ian and Susan. Give George some money so that you all have the same!'**

Susan gives George £_____ .
Ian gives George £_____ .

Culture

Parks

around the world

A ☐ Hyde Park, London, England

There are many parks in London. Hyde Park is a very big one. Many tourists and Londoners go there every day. There are paths for people on bicycles and there are often music concerts in the park.

B ☐ Stanley Park, Vancouver, Canada

Vancouver is a city near the sea and mountains. There is beautiful Stanley Park in the city centre. Over eight million people go there every year. There are First Nations totem poles in the park.

C ☐ Park Güell, Barcelona, Spain

In this park, designed by Antoni Gaudí, there are different houses in different colours. There are also things like a colourful dragon. From the park you can see the city of Barcelona and the sea.

D ☐ Ueno Park, Tokyo, Japan

Ueno Park is an old park in the city of Tokyo and there are hundreds of beautiful cherry trees. In April and May every year, the trees are pink or white.

E ☐ The Iguana Park, Guayaquil, Ecuador

The real name of this small park is Parque Simon Bolivar, but everyone calls it The Iguana Park because it is full of iguanas. The iguanas are very friendly. People in the city go there and feed them.

F ☐ 1 Chapultepec Park, Mexico City, Mexico

This is the biggest city park in Latin America. It's a very important green space in this big city. It has a lake and many museums. People in Mexico City love going there.

1 Look at the photos on page 44. Find these five things and one action.

a dragon | a lake | cherry trees
mountains | sea | feed (verb)

2 🔊 1.52 Read and listen to the article. Match the photos with the texts. Write 1–6 in the boxes.

3 Read the article again. Which parks are these sentences about? Write A–F in the boxes.

0 It isn't a new park. [D]

1 There are museums inside the park. [ ]

2 You can ride your bicycle in the park. [ ]

3 It's possible to see the sea from the park. [ ]

4 You can see animals in this park. [ ]

5 It isn't the only park in that city. [ ]

WRITING
A brochure for your town / city

1 Read Paul's brochure for his town, Alderley Edge. What four things does the town have for visitors?

2 Underline the adjectives that Paul uses to describe the good things in the town.

3 Write a brochure for your town/city. Remember to:

- write a sentence to introduce your town (name, where it is).
- say what there is in the town.
- give some ideas for things to do there.
- write a closing sentence.

4 Now write your brochure (35–50 words).

Come to Alderley Edge!

It's a small, pretty town near Manchester – 30 minutes away by train. Alderley Edge has some great shops and lots of lovely cafés.

- Eat a sandwich in one of the cafés.
- Have lunch or dinner – there are some great restaurants!
- Go to The Edge and see the fantastic view of the countryside.
- Take the train to Manchester – there are excellent museums and brilliant shops there!

Oh, and some famous football players and managers live here. Perhaps you'll see Sir Alex Ferguson!

Alderley Edge – there's something here for everyone!

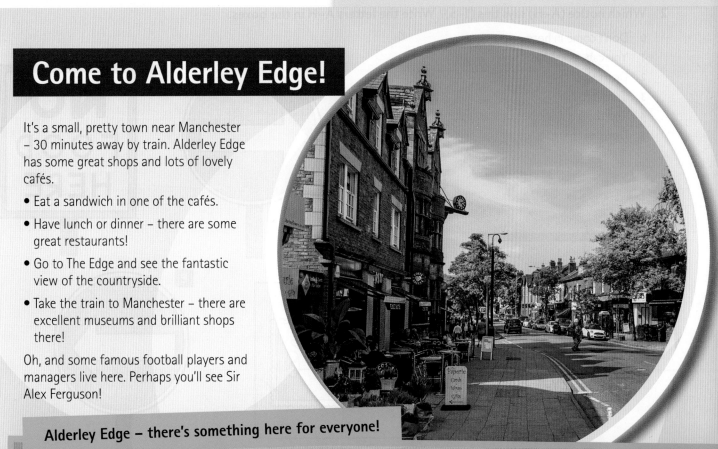

READING AND WRITING
Part 6: Word completion

1 **Read the descriptions of some places in a town. What is the word for each one?**
The first letter is already there. There is one space for each other letter in the word.

0 You catch a train here. s _t_ _a_ _t_ _i_ _o_ _n_

1 There are lots of old and interesting things here. m _ _ _ _ _ _

2 You put your money here. b _ _ _ _

3 Children play here. p _ _ _ _

4 You buy your food here. s _ _ _ _ _ _ _ _ _ _ _

5 You sit and eat here. r _ _ _ _ _ _ _ _ _

Part 1: Matching

2 **Which notice (A–H) says this (1–5)? Write the letters A–H in the boxes.**

0 Don't come in here. | G |

1 You can send letters here.

2 Don't sit here.

3 Turn left.

4 The shop is not open at 5.30 pm.

5 Don't eat here.

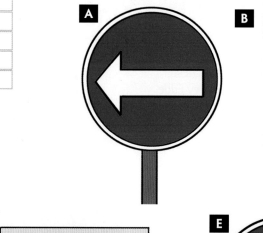

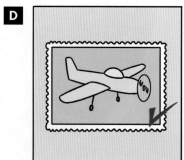

VOCABULARY

1 Complete the sentences with the words in the list. There are two extra words.

bathroom | cooker | garage | garden | grandfather | husband
kitchen | library | on the corner of | opposite | sofa | wife

1 Come and sit on the _____ . Let's watch TV.
2 There's a new fridge in the _____ . It's really big!
3 There's a _____ next to the fridge in the kitchen.
4 The cinema is _____ George Street and Smith Street.
5 There's a bath and a shower in our _____ .
6 She's Mr Graham's _____ . Her name's Pauline.
7 Our house is nice but there isn't a _____ for the car.
8 I love going to the _____ and reading books.
9 The supermarket is _____ the bank.
10 We really love our _____ . He's seventy-two years old now.

/10

GRAMMAR

2 Complete the sentences with the words in the list.

any | my | some | that | there | those

1 Is _____ a library here?
2 Hey! Is _____ your phone? Don't leave it on the desk.
3 How much are _____ black shoes, please?
4 There aren't _____ good films on TV tonight.
5 Are you hungry? Eat _____ sandwiches.
6 Please give me back _____ tablet.

3 Find and correct the mistake in each sentence.

1 There are a really big supermarket in town.
2 Do you like me new phone?
3 I don't like this shoes.
4 Doesn't open the window – it's cold in here!
5 That's bike's Jack.
6 Come and play at us house.

/12

FUNCTIONAL LANGUAGE

4 Complete the missing words.

1 A Hello. Can I h __ __ __ you?
  B Yes, please. H __ __ m __ __ __ are these shoes?
  A £32.99.
  B Great! I'll t __ __ __ them.
2 A Excuse me. W __ __ __ __ is the bank?
  B It's in Green Street. It's n __ __ __ to the supermarket.
  A In Green Street?
  B Yes, walk up here and t __ __ __ left. It's o __ __ __ __ __ __ __ __ a restaurant.

/8

MY SCORE /30

| 22 – 30 |
| 10 – 21 |
| 0 – 9 |

5 | IN MY FREE TIME

B 1

C

D

READING

1 Match the activities in the list with the photos. Write 1–4 in the boxes.

1 listen to music | 2 play sport
3 sing | 4 watch TV

2 Read the newsletter quickly. Which of the activities in Exercise 1 does it talk about?

3 🔊 1.53 **Read and listen to the newsletter. Mark the sentences T (true) or F (false).**

0	Miss Higgins is a Maths teacher.	T
1	The Glee club always sings new songs.	
2	The Glee club gives two concerts every year.	
3	Other students always like the Glee club concerts.	
4	The Glee club is only for Year Seven students.	
5	The Glee club meets two days a week.	

HOME I ABOUT I NEWS I CONTACT

I love Glee Club!

Our school has a Glee club and it's brilliant. I know this because I'm a member! So what is a Glee club? Simple – it's a club for singing and I love singing.

Miss Higgins is the club leader. She chooses the songs and helps us to sing them. She plays the piano, too. She's really cool and she's really kind. She never gets angry with us. She's not even the school Music teacher. She teaches Maths, but she just loves singing.

We often sing popular songs from films but we sometimes sing old songs from the 1960s and 1970s. Three times a year we perform our songs in front of the rest of the school in a special concert. I feel so happy when I'm on stage. The teachers and the other students always cheer when we finish. It feels wonderful.

I love Glee club. Music is a great way to bring people together. You make so many friends at Glee club and not just with people from your school year. Glee club is for all ages.

We meet in the school hall every Tuesday at lunchtime and every Friday after school. Come and join us – we are always happy to see new people!

■ THiNK VALUES ■

Better together or better alone?

1 **It's good to do some things on your own. But some things are better with friends. Look at the table and tick (✓) the answers for you.**

	On my own	With friends
listen to music		
play sport		
play computer games		
watch TV		
do homework		

2 **SPEAKING** Tell your partner.

> I listen to music on my own.

GRAMMAR
Present simple

1 Look at the newsletter on page 49. Complete the sentences with the correct form of the verbs in the list. Then complete the rule.

cheer | ~~love~~ | make | meet | play

0 I _love_ Glee club!

1 You _____ so many friends at Glee club.

2 She _____ the piano, too.

3 We _____ in the school hall.

4 The teachers and other students always _____ when we finish.

> **RULE:** We add **-s** to the base form of the verb when the subject is *he*, [1]_____ or [2]_____ .
>
> **Spelling:** If the verb ends in *consonant + -y*, we change the *y* to an *i* and add *-es*.
>
> E.g. *study* → *stud**ies***
>
> If the verb ends in *-ch, -sh, -ss* or *-x*, we add *-es*.
>
> E.g. *watch* → *watch**es***

2 Write the correct third person form of the verbs in the list. Add *-s*, *-es* or *-ies*.

carry | choose | finish | fly | get | go
help | love | miss | study | teach | watch

> ### Pronunciation
> **Present simple verbs – third person**
> **Go to page 120.** 🔊

Adverbs of frequency

3 Look at the newsletter on page 49 and complete the sentences. Then complete the rule.

0 She _never_ gets angry with us.

1 We _____ sing popular songs.

2 We _____ sing old songs.

3 We're _____ happy to see new people.

> **RULE:**
> [1]_____ [2]_____ [3]_____ _always_
> 0% ——————————→ 100%
>
> With the verb *to be* the adverb of frequency usually comes [4]*before / after* the verb.
>
> With other verbs, the adverb of frequency usually comes [5]*before / after* the verb.

Workbook page 46

VOCABULARY
Free-time activities

1 🔊 1.56 Match the activities in the list with the photos. Write 1–6 in the boxes. Listen and check.

1 chat to friends online | 2 dance
3 do homework | 4 go shopping
5 hang out with friends | 6 play computer games

 A

 B

 C

 D

 E

 F 1

2 Put the words in order to make sentences.

0 computer games / in the morning / I / play / never
   I never play computer games in the morning.

1 often / with friends / hang out / in the park / we

2 sad / I / when / I'm / never / dance

3 goes / with her mum / she / sometimes / shopping

4 after school / always / his homework / does / he

3 Complete the sentences with an adverb of frequency so that they are true for you.

1 I _____ play computer games in the evening.

2 I _____ go shopping with my friends.

3 I _____ do my homework in the morning.

4 I _____ dance in my living room.

5 I _____ chat to my friends online after school.

4 **SPEAKING** Work in pairs. Compare your sentences from Exercise 3. Is anything the same? Compare your sentences with others in the class.

Workbook page 49

LISTENING

1 🔊 1.57 **Listen and write the names under the photos.**

Harry | Julia | Shona | ~~Tim~~

A

B

Tim _____ _____

C

D

_____ _____

2 🔊 1.57 **Listen again and correct the adverb of frequency in each sentence.**

1 Tim sometimes uses the tablet to do his homework.
2 Shona doesn't often watch TV with her family.
3 Julia never plays *Minecraft*™ online with her friends.
4 Harry never uses his phone to text his friends.

3 SPEAKING **Work in pairs. Tell your partner what technology you use and what you use it for. Use adverbs of frequency.**

> *I sometimes use my computer for shopping.*

GRAMMAR
Present simple (negative)

1 **Match the parts of the sentences. Then complete the rule.**

0 I use it to text my friends because   **d**
1 We don't watch TV together in our house; ☐
2 It's free; ☐
3 When Mum calls me for dinner, ☐

a it doesn't cost anything.
b we watch things on the computer.
c I don't want to stop playing.
d it doesn't cost a lot of money.

RULE: We use **don't** and **doesn't** [1] *before / after* the verb to make negative sentences.
I/you/we/they + [2]_____ + base form
he/she/it + [3]_____ + base form
NOT *don't/doesn't* + present simple form
e.g. ~~He doesn't likes music~~

2 **Make the sentences negative.**

0 I like Maths.
I don't like Maths.
1 The lesson finishes at two o'clock.
2 My brother helps me with my homework.
3 We go swimming on Sundays.
4 They watch a lot of TV.
5 My aunt lives in Quito.

3 **Complete the sentences with the correct form of the verbs in brackets.**

1 I sometimes ___play___ (play) computer games with my mum but I _____ (not play) them with my dad.
2 My brother _____ (not do) his homework after school. He _____ (do) it in the morning before school.
3 They often _____ (go) to clubs on Friday night but they _____ (not like) dancing.
4 Susie _____ (not hang out) with her friends after school. She _____ (go) home.
5 I always _____ (listen) to music in the kitchen but my dad _____ (not like) it.

> Workbook page 47

▋THiNK SELF-ESTEEM ▋
What makes me happy?

1 **Tick (✓) what makes you happy.**

	Me	My partner
watch TV		
listen to music		
play computer games		
go shopping		
chat with friends online		
hang out with friends		

2 SPEAKING **Work in pairs. Tell each other two things that make you feel happy and two things that don't. Then tell the class about you and your partner.**

> *I'm happy when I watch TV.*

> *Paolo isn't happy when he goes shopping.*

Does TV control your life?

1 How many hours of TV do you watch every day?

a less than 1   **b** between 1 and 3   **c** more than 3

2 Do you watch TV before school?

a never   **b** sometimes   **c** always

3 Do you watch TV in bed?

a never   **b** sometimes   **c** always

4 Do you watch TV at meal times?

a never   **b** sometimes   **c** always

5 Does your family say that you watch too much TV?

a never   **b** sometimes   **c** always

READING

1 Read the quiz from a teen magazine and choose your answers.

2 **SPEAKING** Work in pairs. Ask and answer the questions with your partner.

3 Work out your score and read your answer. Do you agree with it?

a = 1 point	**b** = 2 points	**c** = 3 points

5 to 9	No, it doesn't. TV doesn't control your life. You control your TV!
10 to 12	TV doesn't control your life but be careful!
13 to 15	Yes, it does! TV controls your life! Turn it off and do something different!

GRAMMAR
Present simple (questions)

1 Look back at the quiz. Put the words in order to make questions. Then complete the rule.

1 your / TV / life / control / does / ?
2 watch / in / you / TV / bed / do / ?

> **RULE:** We use **do** and **does** [1] *before* / *after* the subject to make questions. We use [2]_____ + I/you/we/they + base form and [3]_____ + he/she/it + base form.
>
> To answer we use:
> Yes, I/you/we/they **do**.   No, I/you/we/they **don't**.
> Yes, he/she/it **does**.   No, he/she/it **doesn't**.

2 Choose the correct words.

0 *Do* / *Does* your dad cook?
1 *Do* / *Does* your best friend play football?
2 *Do* / *Does* you like pizza?
3 *Do* / *Does* your parents play computer games?
4 *Do* / *Does* your teacher give you a lot of homework?
5 *Do* / *Does* you hang out with your friends after school?

3 Write questions.

0 you / watch TV with your family
   Do you watch TV with your family?
1 best friend / play tennis
2 your mum and dad / ask for help with housework
3 you / like dogs
4 your mum / take you shopping
5 your friends / listen to music / every day

4 **SPEAKING** Work in pairs. Ask and answer the questions in Exercises 2 and 3.

> *Does your dad cook?*

> *Yes, he does. He sometimes cooks at the weekend.*

> *No, he doesn't. He never cooks.*

Workbook page 47

VOCABULARY
Gadgets

1 🔊 1.58 **Match the gadgets in the list with the pictures. Write 1–8 in the boxes. Listen and check.**

1 e-reader | 2 games console | 3 GPS
4 headphones | 5 laptop | 6 MP3 player
7 smartphone | 8 tablet

A ☐

B ☐

C ☐

D ☐

E ☐ 1

F ☐

2 SPEAKING **Work in pairs. Tell your partner which of these gadgets you use every day.**

💬 I use a tablet every day.

💬 I don't use a laptop every day.

G ☐

3 SPEAKING **Look at the table and make sentences.**

I use / don't use my	tablet games console MP3 player smartphone GPS laptop e-reader headphones	to	play computer games. shop. listen to music. do homework. read books/magazines. talk to my friends. watch TV. find out which way to go.

H ☐

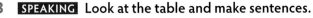

Workbook page 49

WRITING
Days in your life

1 🔊 1.59 **Complete the days of the week with the missing vowels. Listen and check.**

M _o_ nd _a_ y
T _ _ _ sd _ _ y
W _ dn _ _ sd _ _ y
Th _ _ rsd _ _ y
Fr _ _ d _ _ y
S _ _ t _ _ rd _ _ y
S _ _ nd _ _ y

2 **What do you do or not do on different days? Choose three days and make notes.**

○ Sunday — football
○ — no school
○

3 **Write about three days of the week.**

💬 I like Sunday because I always play football and I don't go to school. It's a great day.

The school play

1 **Look at the photos and answer the questions.**

Who can you see in the first photograph?
How do Tom and Ellie feel in photo 2?

2 🔊 1.60 **Now read and listen to the photostory. What does Ruby agree to do?**

RUBY Where are Tom and Ellie?
DAN They're at Drama club. They're in the school play, remember?
RUBY Oh, that's right. They're amazing.
DAN What do you mean?
RUBY To be in a play in front of all the school.

1

DAN Look. Here they are. They don't look very happy.
RUBY Hi, guys. What's wrong?
TOM It's Anna Williams. She's in the play but she's ill.
ELLIE We really need her. The play is on Friday.

2

ELLIE I've got an idea. Ruby, do you want to be in the play? You can have Anna's part.
RUBY Me! No way!
TOM Oh, come on, Ruby. Please. We really need you.
DAN Do it, Ruby. Help your friends.

3

RUBY Oh, OK.
ELLIE I love you, Ruby! Thank you so much.
TOM Yes, you're the best.
RUBY Am I crazy?

4

DEVELOPING SPEAKING

3 ▶ EP3 **Watch to find out how the story continues.**

Does Ruby do the play?

4 ▶ EP3 **Watch again. Correct the false information in the sentences.**

0   Ruby is excited about the play.
    Ruby is nervous about the play.
1   It's four days until the performance.
2   In the play, Ruby wants to speak to the queen.
3   Dan has some bad news for Ruby.
4   Anna Williams is ill.
5   Anna doesn't want to be in the play.

PHRASES FOR FLUENCY

1 Find the expressions 1–4 in the story. Who says them?

1   What's wrong?
2   I've got an idea.
3   No way!
4   Oh, come on.

2 How do you say the expressions in Exercise 1 in your language?

3 Put the sentences in the correct order to make a dialogue.

	MOLLY	Oh, come on, Ben. Please!
	MOLLY	It's my homework. Can you help me with it?
	MOLLY	Very funny, Ben.
1	MOLLY	Hi, Ben. Listen. There's a problem.
	BEN	No way! I always help you with homework.
	BEN	Oh? What's wrong?
	BEN	No! But listen – I've got an idea. Ask Mum!

4 Complete the dialogues with the expressions from Exercise 1.

0   A   I'm bored.
    B   Me too. _____*I've got an idea.*_____ Let's play football in the park.
1   A   Can I talk to you? I've got a problem.
    B   Really? _____
2   A   I don't want to come to the party.
    B   Oh, _____ Jenny. Parties are great!
3   A   Come to the café with me.
    B   _____ I don't like the café.

FUNCTIONS
Encouraging someone

1   Put the words in order to make sentences.

I'm worried. I don't want to do it.

1   are / you / great
2   can / do / it / you
3   worry / don't
4   here / I'm / help / you / to

2   Choose a picture and write a dialogue.

3   SPEAKING Work in pairs. Act out the dialogue.

OBJECTIVES

FUNCTIONS: helping a friend; describing people
GRAMMAR: *have / has got* (positive, negative and questions); countable and uncountable nouns
VOCABULARY: parts of the body; describing people

READING

1 Match the things in the list with the photos. Write 1–6 in the boxes.

1 a woman with a child | 2 a shaved head
3 short black hair | 4 green eyes
5 a doctor and a nurse | 6 long curly hair

2 **SPEAKING** Work in pairs. Complete the sentences. Tell your partner.

My eyes are _____ .
My hair is _____ .
My best friend's eyes are _____ .
My mum's hair is _____ .

> My eyes are brown.

3 🔊 1.61 Read and listen to the article. What's wrong with Delaney?

4 Read the article again. Match the parts of the sentences.

0 Delaney is 11 and the girls and boys — *e*
1 The doctors say that she's got
2 She's in hospital for months and this
3 Delaney hasn't got any hair
4 Kamryn shaves her head and
5 The teachers at the school don't want Kamryn

a a terrible illness.
b so Delaney is really happy.
c and her friend Kamryn wants to help her.
d at school with a shaved head.
e in her class like her a lot.
f is difficult for her, but she's strong.

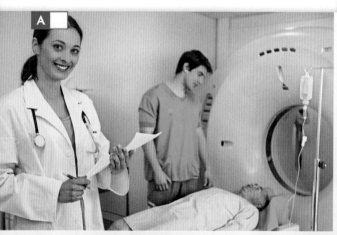

A real friend

Delaney Clements is 11. She's got a big smile and beautiful hair. She's a very active girl and loves sport. Delaney is very popular with her classmates. Her best friend is a girl called Kamryn. She's in Delaney's class.

One day Delaney is very tired and feels bad. Her mum and dad take her to hospital. The doctors check the girl. They say that Delaney is very ill. She's got cancer. Her parents are very worried.

Delaney is in hospital for months. It's a very difficult time for her, but she often smiles. The doctors and nurses like her a lot. She's a very strong girl.

Delaney looks very different now. She hasn't got any hair. But she's got a real friend, Kamryn. Kamryn talks to her parents. She wants to help Delaney. She wants to look like Delaney. Delaney feels different from her classmates. Kamryn shaves her head. When Delaney sees her friend without hair, she's very happy. She's got a really good friend. Now Delaney isn't alone.

But there is a terrible surprise for Kamryn the next day at school. Her teachers say it isn't OK to have a shaved head. They don't want Kamryn to go to school with a shaved head.

A lot of people don't understand the teachers, and they tell the school what they think. The newspapers have got lots of stories about the two girls.

In the end, the teachers say it's OK. Kamryn goes back to school.

■ THiNK VALUES ■

Helping a friend

SPEAKING How can you help a friend in these situations? Work in pairs. Use the suggestions in the list and your own ideas.

I help him/her study. | I talk to him/her.
I make him/her a sandwich. | I lend him/her my tablet.
I give him/her a hug.

1 My friend is sad.
2 My friend gets a bad mark in his/her Maths test.
3 My friend is hungry with nothing to eat.
4 My friend's computer is broken.
5 My friend has got a problem at school.

GRAMMAR

have / has got (positive and negative)

1 Look at the article on page 57. Choose the correct form of *have got* in the sentences. Then complete the rule and the table.

1 She *'ve got / 's got* a big smile.

2 She *haven't got / hasn't got* any hair.

3 The newspapers *has got / have got* lots of stories about the two girls.

> **RULE:** We use *have / has* (+ *not*) +
> 1_____ to talk about possession.

Positive	Negative
I/you/we/they**'ve got (have got)**	I/you/we/they 1_____ **got (have not got)**
he/she/it**'s got** (2_____ **got)**	he/she/it **hasn't got (has not got)**

2 Complete the sentences with the correct form of *have got*.

0 This computer is £700. I ___*haven't got*___ the money to buy it.

1 My best friend Tony _____ any sisters, but he _____ two brothers.

2 I _____ a tablet but I really want one.

3 I _____ a new smartphone. Here's my new number.

4 James and Annie _____ a car, but they've got bikes.

5 Lara _____ a big family. She _____ three sisters and one brother.

Workbook page 54

VOCABULARY
Parts of the body

1 🔊 1.62 Label the picture with the words in the list. Listen and check.

~~arm~~ | body | ear | eye | face
foot | hand | leg | mouth | nose

2 **SPEAKING** Work in pairs. Look at the picture and labels for 30 seconds. Then cover the words. Point to the parts of the body and test your partner.

> What's this?

> It's an arm.

Workbook page 57

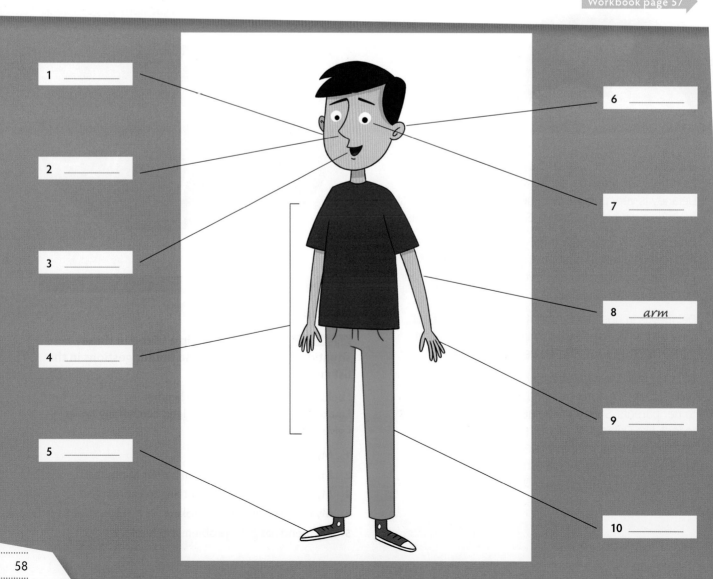

1 _____

2 _____

3 _____

4 _____

5 _____

6 _____

7 _____

8 ___*arm*___

9 _____

10 _____

LISTENING

1 Which of these sentences do you agree with?

1 It's good to give little presents to your friends sometimes.
2 A friendship band is a great present.
3 I really like friendship bands.

2 Look at the photo and read the text. Then answer the question.

Why do people like friendship bands?

3 ◀))1.63 Listen to an interview with 12-year-old Ella Winston. What are her hobbies?

4 ◀))1.63 Listen again and complete the sentences.

0 Ella's got five or six _friendship bands_ .
1 She's got two or three _____ .
2 In total, she's got about _____ friends.
3 She spends about _____ a day making friendship bands.
4 The rubber bands are not _____ .
5 Sometimes she uses seven or eight different _____ .

Friendship bands

David Beckham has got one. The Duchess of Cambridge has got one. Harry Styles from One Direction has got one. And millions of other young and old people have got them, too. Friendship bands are popular all over the world. They are fun and look cool. And, they help us to think of our friends.

GRAMMAR
have / has got (questions)

1 Match the questions and answers. Complete the table.

1 Have you got a hobby? ☐
2 Has your sister got a smartphone? ☐
3 Have your teachers got friendship bands? ☐

a Yes, she has.
b No, they haven't.
c Yes, I have.

Questions	Short answers
Have I/you/we/they **got**?	Yes, I/you/we/they **have**. No, I/you/we/they **haven't**. (**have not**)
¹_____ he/she/it **got**?	Yes, she/he/it ²_____ . No, she/he/it ³_____ . (**has not**)

2 Answer the questions.

1 Have you got a TV in your bedroom?
2 Have you got a TV in your kitchen?
3 Have you got a garden?
4 Have you got a big family?
5 Has your best friend got a big family?
6 Have you got a mobile phone with lots of songs on it?

3 SPEAKING Walk around the classroom. Ask and answer the questions in Exercise 2. Find someone with a 'yes' answer for each question and write down their name.

Countable and uncountable nouns

4 Complete the table with the words in the list and *a/an* or *some*. Then complete the rule.

apple | ~~arm~~ | ~~bikes~~ | chairs | colour | ~~friend~~
fun | hobby | money | pens | ~~time~~ | work

Countable (singular)	Countable (plural)	Uncountable
an arm *a friend*	*some bikes*	*some time*

RULE: You can count **countable** nouns: one, two, three, etc. + **countable** noun (e.g. *two friends, four bikes*).

With singular **countable** nouns, we use *a* or ¹_____ .

You can't count **uncountable** nouns (e.g. *time*).

With **uncountable** nouns and plural **countable** nouns, we use ²_____ .

Workbook pages 54–55 ➤

READING

1 🔊 1.64 **Read and listen to the dialogue. What's the surprise for Olivia?**

OLIVIA Hey, Chloe. How are you?

CHLOE Hi, Olivia. I'm fine. How are you?

OLIVIA I'm happy. You know my brother, Patrick, right? Well, he's got a new friend. He's really cool.

CHLOE Really? Who is he? What does he look like?

OLIVIA Well, he's got black hair. It's short and it's curly.

CHLOE Is he tall or short?

OLIVIA Quite tall, and good-looking. He's got brown eyes and he wears glasses.

CHLOE Brown eyes and glasses?

OLIVIA Erm … yes, and he's got a very nice smile. He's so friendly.

CHLOE I know.

OLIVIA You know?

CHLOE He likes football and tennis and his name's Freddie, right?

OLIVIA That's right, but … but …

CHLOE And he's got a sister?

OLIVIA How do you know?

CHLOE Freddie's … my brother!

OLIVIA No way!

2 **SPEAKING** **Which picture shows Freddie? Tell a partner.**

He's number … He's got …

VOCABULARY
Describing people (1)

1 **Look at the words in the list. Write them under the correct headings. Some words can go under more than one heading.**

~~blue~~ | ~~grey~~ | ~~long~~ | curly | short | black | blonde
red | brown | wavy | straight | green

eye colour	hair colour	hair style
blue	*grey*	*long*

2 **SPEAKING** **Work in pairs. Use the words in Exercise 1 to describe the people in the photos.**

James Rodriguez | Pink

George Clooney | Shakira

James Rodriguez has got …

Pink has got …

Workbook page 57

Pronunciation
Long vowel sound /eɪ/
Go to page 120. 🔊

Describing people (2)

3 ◀)) 1.67 **Match the words in the list with the pictures. Write 1–7 in the boxes. Listen and check.**

1 beard | 2 earring | 3 glasses
4 moustache | 5 short | 6 smile | 7 tall

FUNCTIONS
Describing people

1 **Complete the dialogue with answers a–d.**

A I'm thinking of a famous footballer.

B What does he look like?

A ⁰ *d*

B What's he like?

A ¹ _____

B Is he British?

A ² _____

B Is it Gareth Bale?

A ³ _____

a He's really nice.

b Yes, he is.

c Yes, it is.

d He's tall and strong. He's got short brown hair and a lovely smile.

2 **SPEAKING** **Work in pairs. Think of a famous person. Ask and answer questions to guess who he/she is.**

> I'm thinking of a famous female singer.

> What does she look like?

4 ◀)) 1.68 **Put the words in the correct order to make sentences. Listen and check. Then match each sentence with a picture in Exercise 3.**

0 smile / a / she's / nice / very / got   ☐ *F*
   She's got a very nice smile.

1 she / glasses / wears   ☐

2 moustache / got / a / he's   ☐

3 he's / beard / a / got   ☐

4 got / earring / right / she's / her / ear / an / in   ☐

5 is not short / she / quite tall / she's   ☐

5 ◀)) 1.69 **Complete the dialogue with the missing words. Listen and check.**

A I've got a new friend. His name's Eric.

B What does he look like?

A He's got short brown ⁰h *air* _____ , blue ¹e_____ and he wears ²g_____ .

B Is he tall or ³s_____ ?

A He isn't very tall.

B Is he nice?

A He's very nice and friendly. He's got a nice ⁴s_____ .

6 **SPEAKING** **Work in pairs. Act out the dialogue.**

> Workbook page 57 ▶

■ TRAIN TO THiNK ■
Attention to detail

1 **SPEAKING** **Work in pairs. Student A: Go to page 127. Student B: Go to page 128. Describe the people in your picture. Find the six differences.**

2 **SPEAKING** **Tell others in the class what differences you have found.**

> In picture A, the waiter has got grey hair. In picture B, …

Culture

Welcoming people around the world

Western countries

What do you do when you see someone you know? Do you smile? Do you say hello? Do you touch the other person? Here are some ideas for travellers. They tell you how people in different countries and cultures welcome each other. Do you do different things in your country?

In many countries in Asia, people bow their heads when they greet each other. This shows respect. In Thailand, people put their hands together and bow. This is called the 'wai' and is a very old tradition.

In Mongolia, people give a 'hada' to guests who visit their home. This is a piece of silk. When you get a 'hada', hold it in both hands. This also shows respect.

The Maori people in New Zealand rub noses together when they meet. This is called the 'hongi'.

In Western countries, many people shake hands when they greet each other. Sometimes they just smile and say something like 'Hello!' or 'Hi!'

In many countries around the world, friends greet by kissing on the cheek. In some countries they do it on one cheek, in others they do it on two cheeks and in some they kiss cheeks three times.

1 Look at the photos on page 62. Find these things or actions.

bow their heads | kiss | a piece of silk
put their hands together | rub noses
shake hands | smile | touch

2 What do the photos show?

A people saying hello
B people helping people
C people saying thank you

3 🔊 1.70 Read and listen to the article. Write the names of the places under the photos.

4 Read the article again. Mark the sentences T (true) or F (false).

0 The bow is a tradition in Asia. `T`
1 In Thailand, people rub their noses to say hello.
2 When you get a 'hada', don't hold it in one hand.
3 Maori people use the 'hongi' to say hello.
4 In Western countries, people never shake hands.
5 People only greet others with a kiss in Western countries.
6 In some countries, people kiss three times.

5 SPEAKING Discuss with a partner.

1 Which is your favourite way of welcoming people described in the text?
2 How do you welcome people in your country?

WRITING
Describing a friend

1 Read the text. Tick (✓) the correct picture of James.

1

2

3

My best friend is called James Webb. He's quite tall. He's got short curly black hair and he wears glasses. He's in my class at school and he always helps me in my lessons. After school we always play football in the park and at the weekends we often go swimming together. He's a really friendly boy and he's got a very nice smile. He's very popular and everyone likes him. But I'm his best friend!

2 Read the text again. Complete the notes about James.

Appearance: hair – _____ , _____
and _____
wears _____
tall
has got a nice smile

Personality: friendly – (nice smile!)
_____ – (has got lots of friends)

3 Think about your best friend. Make notes.

Appearance:

Personality:

4 Answer the questions about your best friend.

1 What's his/her name?
2 How do you know him/her?
3 Why do you like him/her?
4 What do you do together?

5 Use your notes from Exercises 3 and 4 to write a short text (35–50 words) about your best friend.

READING AND WRITING
Part 4: Multiple-choice reading comprehension

1 Read the article about a school club.

For each sentence choose the correct answer A, B or C.

Our school has a LEGO club and it's great fun. It's on Tuesday and Thursday lunchtime from 12 pm to 1 pm. I'm a member of the club and so is my best friend Ally.

Mr Thomas is the club organiser and the club is in his classroom, 3T. He's got five big boxes of LEGO bricks.

Every week he spends the first 15 minutes showing us different ways to build things. We then practise this for the rest of the time. He sometimes organises competitions. The prize is always a small box of LEGO.

This month there is a competition for all schools in the UK to build a LEGO classroom. The prize is a school trip to LEGOLAND. I hope our LEGO club wins!

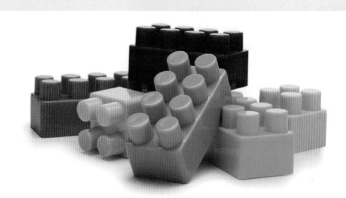

0 The LEGO club is at _____ .
A the library   B the museum   C⃝ school

1 The club meets _____ times a week.
A two   B three   C four

2 The meetings are for _____ .
A 15 minutes   B 30 minutes   C 60 minutes.

3 Mr Thomas teaches in _____ 3T.
A school   B classroom   C box

4 Mr Thomas shows the students how to make things with LEGO for _____ .
A fifteen minutes   B thirty minutes   C one hour

5 The prize for Mr Thomas' competition is a _____ .
A LEGO model   B LEGO book   C trip to LEGOLAND

Part 9: Guided writing

2 Read the email from your pen friend Sophie.

From: Sophie
To:

Please tell me about the things you do in your free time. What do you do after school? What do you do at the weekend?

Write an email to Sophie and answer the questions. Write 25–35 words.

TEST YOURSELF

VOCABULARY

1 **Complete the sentences with the words in the list. There are two extra words.**

arm | beard | curly | dance | do | earrings | eyes | glasses | go | headphones | out | short

1   No, I can't go out. I need to _____ my homework.
2   I always use _____ when I listen to music at home.
3   She's got a friendship band on her left _____ .
4   It's OK music, but you can't _____ to it.
5   My eyes aren't very good. That's why I wear _____ .
6   Let's _____ shopping tomorrow afternoon.
7   He's got a big black _____ and a moustache.
8   I like her hair. It's long and _____ .
9   He's got really nice blue _____ .
10 I want to go and hang _____ with my friends this evening.

/10

GRAMMAR

2 **Put the words in order to make sentences or questions.**

1   like / shopping / she / doesn't
2   never / they / to / listen / rock music
3   many / got / you / DVDs / haven't
4   she / money / got / has / lots of
5   always / I / late / to school / get
6   lots / got / you / of / have / books
7   usually / are / tired / on Sunday evenings / we

3 **Find and correct the mistake in each sentence.**

1   I go often to the cinema.
2   They listen not to music.
3   He play computer games all the time.
4   Have he got a moustache?
5   She don't do her homework.
6   I've got a work to do tonight.
7   You have got a big family?

/14

FUNCTIONAL LANGUAGE

4 **Write the missing words.**

1   **A**   There's a new girl in our class.
    B   Oh? What's she _____ ?
    A   She's nice. But she _____ talk a lot.
    B   Oh. And what does she _____ like?
    A   She's tall and she's got long black hair.

2   **A**   Are you OK?
    B   No. I can't do this homework.
    A   Don't _____ . I can help you.
    B   Oh, thanks. You're _____ !
    A   No problem. I'm here to _____ you.

/6

MY SCORE   **/30**

| 22 – 30 |
| 10 – 21 |
| 0 – 9 |

7 SPORTING LIFE

READING

1 Match the sports in the list with the photos. Write 1–4 in the boxes.

1 football | 2 golf
3 gymnastics | 4 skateboarding

2 Look at Exercise 1. In which sports do you do these actions?

1 kick   4 hit
2 push   5 spin
3 jump   6 do somersaults

3 ◀))2.02 Read and listen to the article. Write the names under the photos in Exercise 1.

Tillman | Xavier
Nikolai | The Firecrackers

4 Read the article again. Tick (✓) the correct box for each sentence.

	right	wrong	doesn't say
0 Nikolai only uses his feet and legs to stop the ball from falling.		✓	
1 Nikolai can do this for more than a day.			
2 Xavier likes to read golf magazines.			
3 Xavier's hero is Rory McIlroy.			
4 Tillman lives in England.			
5 Tillman doesn't need help to get on the skateboard.			
6 The Firecrackers are a group of friends.			
7 The Firecrackers are very entertaining.			

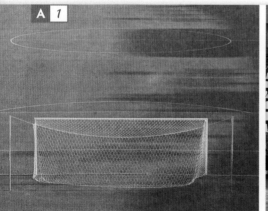

A **1**

B

C

D

They're good!

Nikolai Kutsenko

Nikolai Kutsenko can do amazing things with a football. He can kick a ball well … but he can also keep the ball in the air with his feet, legs and head. Lots of footballers can do this. But can they do it for 24 hours and 30 minutes without stopping? Nikolai can and it's a world record!

Xavier Good

Xavier Good is three years old. He's a little boy and there are a lot of things he can't do. He can't read or write, for example. But Xavier can do something special. He can hit a golf ball. He can hit it a long way. And he can hit it into the hole. Is he the next Rory McIlroy?

Tillman

Skateboarding is a popular hobby with teenagers everywhere. But in the USA, people always stop and watch a skateboarder called Tillman. Tillman is an English bulldog but he can skateboard like a person. He jumps on the skateboard and pushes it with his feet. And he's off!

The Firecrackers

The Firecrackers are a group of young girls who do gymnastics. They can jump and spin and do somersaults like other gymnasts, but the Firecrackers use a skipping rope at the same time. Some people call their routine a dance, not a sport, because they use music. But some gymnastics routines use music, too. Everyone agrees that the girls are athletes, and that their routines are fun and amazing to watch.

▌THiNK VALUES ▌

The importance of sport

1 **Why do people do sport? Read the reasons below and add two more of your own. Put these reasons in order of importance. Write 1–8 in the boxes.**

- [ ] It's fun.
- [ ] You can make friends.
- [ ] It's good to win.
- [ ] It's easy.
- [ ] It's healthy.
- [ ] It's exciting.
- [ ] _____
- [ ] _____

2 **SPEAKING Compare your ideas with others in the class.**

> People do sport because it's fun.

GRAMMAR
can (ability)

1 Look at the article on page 67 and complete the sentences. Then complete the rule and the table.

1 They _____ jump.

2 _____ they do it for 24 hours?

3 He _____ read or write.

> **RULE:** We use ¹_____ to talk about ability.
> The negative form is ²_____ .
> We don't use *do/does* with *can* in questions or negative forms.

Positive	Negative
I/you/we/he/she/it/they **can** jump.	I/you/we/he/she/it/they ¹_____ (**cannot**) jump.
Questions ²_____ I/you/we/he/she/it/they jump?	**Short answers** Yes, I/you/we/he/she/it/they **can**. No, I/you/we/he/she/it/they **can't**.

2 Write sentences about John with *can* or *can't*.

0 swim ✓
  John can swim.
1 sing ✗
2 cook ✓
3 speak French ✗
4 dance ✗
5 ride a bike ✓

> ## Pronunciation
> **Long vowel sound /ɔː/**
> **Go to page 121.** 🔊

3 Look at the activities in the list. Tick (✓) the things you can do.

☐ hit a golf ball
☐ do a somersault
☐ skateboard
☐ throw a ball 20 metres
☐ spell your name in English
☐ count to 20 in English
☐ say the alphabet in less than 30 seconds
☐ play the guitar
☐ make a cake
☐ jump high

4 **SPEAKING** Work in pairs. Ask and answer questions.

> *Can you count to 20 in English?*

> *Yes, I can. 1, 2, 3, 4, …*

Workbook page 64 ➤

VOCABULARY
Sport

1 🔊 2.05 Match the words in the list with the photos. Write 1–8 in the boxes. Listen and check.

1 cycle │ 2 do tae kwon do │ 3 go surfing
4 ice-skate │ 5 play basketball
6 play tennis │ 7 play volleyball │ 8 snowboard

2 **SPEAKING** Work in pairs. Which of these sports *can/can't* you do? Tell your partner.

> *I can ice-skate but I can't play volleyball.*

Workbook page 67 ➤

A ☐ B ☐ C ☐ D ☐ E ☐ F ☐ G 1 H ☐

VOCABULARY
Telling the time

1 ◀)) 2.06 **Match the times in the list with the clocks. Write 1–4 in the boxes. Listen and check.**

1 It's three o'clock. | 2 It's half past eight.
3 It's quarter past ten. | 4 It's quarter to one.

A 3   **B** ☐   **C** ☐   **D** ☐

2 SPEAKING **Write the times under the clocks. Then ask and answer in pairs.**

What's the time?   It's quarter past four.

0 _It's quarter past four._   1 _____

2 _____   3 _____

Workbook page 67 ➡

LISTENING

1 ◀)) 2.07 **Listen to a phone call between Sam and Lucy. When do they decide to go surfing?**

2 ◀)) 2.07 **Listen again and tick (✓) the sports you hear.**

☐	a	tennis
✓	b	surfing
☐	c	rugby
☐	d	volleyball
☐	e	golf
☐	f	basketball

3 ◀)) 2.07 **Listen again. Match the clocks and the sentences. Write 1–8 in the boxes.**

1 The volleyball match starts at …
2 The volleyball match finishes at …
3 The golf lesson starts at …
4 The golf lesson finishes at …
5 It gets dark at …
6 The basketball match finishes at …
7 The basketball match starts at …
8 The time now is …

4 **Think of four things you do every day. Draw the time that you do them on clocks in your notebook.**

5 SPEAKING **Work in pairs. Look at your partner's clock. Guess what he/she does at each time. Use the things below or your own ideas.**

get up   **have breakfast**
start school   play football   *do your homework*
have dinner   **go to bed**

Do you get up at half past six?

Do you have breakfast at …?

Do you …?

■ THiNK SELF-ESTEEM ■

My time cake

1 **Look at the example of a time cake then draw a time cake for you.**

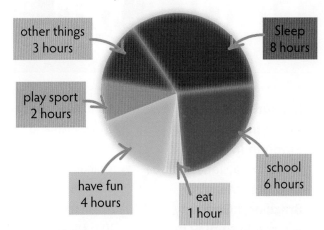

other things 3 hours   Sleep 8 hours
play sport 2 hours   school 6 hours
have fun 4 hours   eat 1 hour

2 SPEAKING **Work in pairs. Talk about your time cake.**

1 Are you happy with your time cake?
2 Would you like to change it? How?

3 SPEAKING **Draw your ideal time cake. Compare with your partner.**

A ☐   B ☐   C 1   D ☐
E ☐   F ☐   G ☐   H ☐

READING

1 **SPEAKING** Work in pairs. Discuss these questions.

  1 What important football matches can you think of?

  2 Who are the champions of
    a your country   **b** the world?

  3 Look at the photos. What do you think is special about this football match?

2 **◀))2.08** Read and listen to the article. Which two teams play 'the other final' and who wins?

3 Read the article again. Put the events in the correct order.

☐	a	Matthijs organises a football match.
☐	b	Germany and Brazil play in the World Cup final.
1	c	The Dutch team aren't in the World Cup final.
☐	d	Montserrat and Bhutan play a game of football.
☐	e	Matthijs de Jongh has a plan.
☐	f	The Montserrat national team flies to Bhutan.

4 **SPEAKING** Work in pairs. Choose two teams for your perfect 'other final'.

  1 Where do they play?

  2 Who wins?

  3 Who scores the goals?

The Other Final

It's 30th June 2002. In the International Stadium in Yokohama, Japan, two great teams, Brazil and Germany, are ready to play in the World Cup final.

4,500 kilometres away in the Changlimithang Stadium in Thimphu, Bhutan, there is another football match: Bhutan vs. Montserrat. Bhutan are number 202 in the world, Montserrat are 203. They are the bottom two teams in the world.

It's Matthijs de Jongh's idea. He's a Dutch businessman. He can't watch his national team, the Netherlands, because they are not at this World Cup. He's sad but then he thinks about people from other countries. What about teams that never play in the World Cup? He organises 'the other final' and asks the national teams of Bhutan and Montserrat to play. The Montserrat team fly from the Caribbean to the Himalayan mountains of Bhutan. Thousands of people watch the match. Bhutan win 4–0, but everyone decides that football is the real winner.

After their game, both teams sit down with the rest of the world and enjoy the real World Cup final.

VOCABULARY
Months and seasons

1 ◀))2.09 **Put the months in the correct order. Write 1–12 in the boxes. Listen and check.**

☐ June	☐ September	☐ February
☐ May	☐ October	☐ July
☐ March	*1* January	☐ August
☐ November	☐ April	☐ December

2 **What months are in these seasons in the UK?**

winter

spring

summer

autumn

→ Workbook page 67

GRAMMAR
Prepositions of time

1 **Read the example sentences and complete the rule with *in*, *at* and *on*.**

The football match starts **at** 3 pm.
My birthday is **in** March. It's **in** spring.
The party is **on** Friday.

> **RULE:** With times we use ¹_____ .
> For months and seasons we use ²_____ .
> For days of the week we use ³_____ .

2 ◀))2.10 **Do you know when these sporting events are? Guess, then listen and check.**

> *The World Cup final is usually in June or July.*

~~The World Cup final~~
The Australian Open Tennis
The French Open Tennis
The Summer Olympics
The Winter Olympics
Wimbledon

→ Workbook page 65

VOCABULARY
Ordinal numbers

1 **Look at the article on page 70. Complete the sentence with the missing date.**

It's _____ June 2002. In the International Stadium in Yokohama, …

> **LOOK!** When we say the date, we usually say **the 7th of** March but we write **7th** March.

2 ◀))2.11 **Match the numbers with the words. Listen, check and repeat.**

1st	*h*	9th	☐	a	sixth	i	thirtieth
2nd	☐	10th	☐	b	eleventh	j	eighth
3rd	☐	11th	☐	c	thirteenth	k	thirty-first
4th	☐	12th	☐	d	third	l	twelfth
5th	☐	13th	☐	e	tenth	m	second
6th	☐	20th	☐	f	fifth	n	twentieth
7th	☐	30th	☐	g	ninth	o	seventh
8th	☐	31st	☐	h	first	p	fourth

3 **SPEAKING Write three important dates for you. Tell your partner about them.**

> *My sister's birthday is on the 8th of May.*

> *Our school's Sports Day is on the 20th of June.*

→ Workbook page 67

WRITING
My favourite sportsperson

1 **Think of your favourite sportsperson and answer the questions.**

1 Who is he/she?
2 Where is he/she from?
3 What sport does he/she do?
4 What sort of things can he/she do?
5 Are there any things he/she can't do?
6 Why do you like him/her?

2 **SPEAKING Work in pairs. Tell your partner about your favourite sportsperson.**

3 **Write a short text (50–70 words) about your favourite sportsperson. Use your ideas from Exercises 1 and 2.**

The big match

1 Look at the photos and answer the questions.

Where are they in photo 2?
What happens to the TV?

2 🔊 2.12 Now read and listen to the photostory. Who does Tom want to win?

1

TOM It's the big match this afternoon. Why don't we all watch it together?
RUBY Great idea!
TOM OK. You call Ellie and I can call Dan. About 3.30 at my place!
RUBY Hmm, I've got some stuff to do first, but I think 3.30 is OK.

2

MAN ON TV Welcome to today's match. We're here live in London!
ELLIE It's so exciting.
DAN I know. I love football.
TOM The US can win this. I know it. Go USA!
RUBY No way, Tom. Go England!

3

RUBY Hey. The TV screen. Is it broken? We can't see anything.
ELLIE Where's the match? We want to watch the match!
DAN Come on, Tom. Do something! The match starts in a few minutes!
TOM Just a minute. Let me try and fix it.

4

ELLIE Oh, no. Now the screen's black.
DAN Now what do we do?
TOM It's no big deal. I'm sure I can fix it.
RUBY This is terrible!

DEVELOPING SPEAKING

3 ▶ EP4 **Watch to find out how the story continues.**

1 What sports do Ruby, Ellie and Dan play?

2 Who wins the match on television?

4 ▶ EP4 **Watch again. Choose the correct answers.**

0 Who offers to help Tom?
(A) Dan
B Ruby
C Ellie

1 Where is the table tennis table?
A in the living room
B in Tom's bedroom
C in the games room

2 Who wins the table tennis game?
A Dan
B Ruby
C Ellie

3 Where is the basketball hoop?
A in the garage
B outside
C in the games room

4 Where does Tom find the others?
A in the kitchen
B in the games room
C in the garden

5 Who wins the big game?
A the USA
B England
C We don't know.

PHRASES FOR FLUENCY

1 Find the expressions 1–4 in the story. Who says them?

1 … stuff.
2 Now what …?
3 It's no big deal.
4 I'm sure …

2 How do you say the expressions in Exercise 1 in your language?

3 Put the sentences in the correct order to make a dialogue.

	ANDY	You know, books and things. I need them for school. Now what do I do?
	ANDY	With no books? Are you sure?
1	ANDY	I haven't got my school stuff with me.
	SUE	What school stuff?
	SUE	Oh, it's no big deal. You can go to lessons without books.
	SUE	Yes, I'm sure you can. Come on, we're late.

4 Complete the dialogues with the expressions from Exercise 1.

0 A Who is that woman?
B _I'm sure_ she's a famous actress. I can't remember her name.

1 A Come to the shops with me.
B I can't. I've got a lot of _____ to do at home.

2 A My computer is broken.
B But we need the Internet! _____ ?

3 A I can't find my phone.
B _____ . You can use my phone.

FUNCTIONS
Making suggestions

1 Complete the sentences from the story. Use the words and phrases in the list.

How about | Let's | Why don't

1 _____ we all watch it together?
2 _____ go and play table tennis.
3 _____ playing another game?

2 Complete the suggestions.

1 A I'm bored.
B _____ watching a film?

2 A There's nothing to do.
B _____ we go for a walk?

3 A I'm hungry.
B _____ make some sandwiches.

3 SPEAKING **Work in pairs. Act out the dialogues in Exercise 2.**

4 SPEAKING **Make two new dialogues. Use these words for speaker A.**

thirsty
tired

8 DANCE TO THE MUSIC

READING

1 Match the words in the list with the photos. Write 1–5 in the boxes.

   1 a concert | 2 a musician | 3 a singer
   4 a trumpet | 5 a violin

2 Look at the photos on page 75. They show a concert. Where is it?

   1 in a train station
   2 in a concert hall
   3 in a supermarket
   4 in a school

3 Do you use Twitter? What do you know about Tweets?

4 ◄)) 2.13 Read and listen to the Tweets. Answer the questions.

   0 How does Alex feel at 09.44?
   bored
   1 How many musicians are playing at 09.48?
   2 How do the people in the supermarket feel at 09.49?
   3 How many people are singing in the concert at 09.50?
   4 How does Alex feel at 09.51?
   5 What are the musicians doing at 09.55?

A

B

C 1

D

E

Home   Profile   Messages

Search

#musicinsupermarket

Alex Smith
#AlexSmith

09.44
Saturday am. In the supermarket with Mum. We're doing some shopping. Boring! People are walking around. I'm listening to music on my phone.

09.47
Hey, something is happening. A woman is sitting on a chair and she's playing a violin. What's this?! It's a flash mob in the supermarket!

09.48
Wow. This is fantastic! Now about ten men and women are standing here and they're playing music on violins and trumpets and things.

09.49
I'm looking at the other people in the supermarket. They're surprised but they like the music. They aren't thinking about food now!

09.50
Now four people are singing! They're giving a concert but they aren't wearing special clothes. Why is this happening? I don't know!

09.51
Mum says that the music is Handel??!! She isn't shopping now – she's standing with me and we're listening. I'm not bored now!

09.53
Lots of people are taking out their phones and recording the concert. Other people are tweeting, like me! And a little girl is dancing.

09.55
OK, it's over. All the people here are smiling and talking about the music. The musicians and singers are leaving. What a great morning!

■ THiNK VALUES ■

Music

1 **SPEAKING** Tick (✓) the places where you listen to music. Tell your partner. How many are the same?

☐ in my room	☐ on the bus/train
☐ outside	☐ in the shops
☐ at school	☐ another place (Where?)

> *I listen to music in my room, outside and on the bus.*

2 **What are your reasons for listening to music? Write 1–3 in the boxes: 3 = a very important reason, 2 = an important reason, 1 = not an important reason.**

☐ It makes me happy.

☐ I can listen with friends.

☐ It's free.

☐ I can forget my problems.

☐ I can dance to it.

3 **SPEAKING** Work in groups. Compare your ideas.

GRAMMAR
Present continuous

1 Look at the examples of the present continuous. Underline other examples in the Tweets on page 75. Then choose the correct words to complete the rule and the table.

I'm **listening** to music on my phone.
A woman **is sitting** on a chair.
They **aren't wearing** special clothes.
Why is this **happening**?

> **RULE:** We use the present continuous to talk about things that [1]*happen every day / are happening now*. We form the present continuous with the present tense of [2] *to be / to have* and the *-ing* form of the main verb.

Positive	Negative	Question + short answer
I'm **(am)** listen**ing**.	I'm **not (am not)** listen**ing**.	[5]_____ I listen**ing**? Yes, I [6]_____ . No, I'**m not**.
You/We/They [1]_____ **(are)** listen**ing**.	You/We/They **aren't (are not)** [3]_____ .	[7]_____ you/we/they listen**ing**? Yes, you/we/they **are**. No, you/we/they [8]_____ .
He/She/It [2]_____ **(is)** listen**ing**.	He/She/It [4]_____ **(is not)** listen**ing**.	[9]_____ he/she/it [10]_____ ? Yes, he/she/it [11]_____ . No, he/she/it **isn't**.

2 Look at the pictures. Then write a name to complete the sentences.

0   _Jake_ is singing.
1   _____ are sitting.
2   _____ is taking a photo.
3   _____ is talking on the phone.
4   _____ is leaving.
5   _____ is reading.
6   _____ are dancing.
7   _____ is standing and cheering.
8   _____ is wearing a blue hat and smiling.
9   _____ is running.

> **LOOK!** Spelling
> si**ng** – sing**ing**   li**ve** – li**ving**
> sw**im** – swi**mming**

3 Write the correct *-ing* form of these verbs.

0   come   _coming_
1   take   _____
2   get   _____
3   shop   _____
4   make   _____
5   watch   _____
6   play   _____
7   study   _____

4 Complete the sentences with the verbs from Exercise 3 in the correct form.

0   A   Come on, Jane, we're late!
    B   OK, Sam, I _'m coming_ now!
1   A   Where's Molly?
    B   She's in the living room. She _____ TV.
2   A   Is Jacob here?
    B   No, he isn't. He _____ computer games in his bedroom.
3   A   Can I talk to Mike, please?
    B   Sorry, he's in town. He _____ for shoes.
4   A   Let's go home now.
    B   You're right. It _____ late. Look, it's almost ten o'clock.
5   A   Is your dad in the kitchen?
    B   Yes, he is! He _____ a cake!
6   A   Where's Alex?
    B   He _____ the dog for a walk in the park.
7   A   So, your sister is in the USA.
    B   That's right. She _____ at a university there.

Workbook page 72 ➜

Sally

Linda   Greg

Jake   Debbie   Paula   Steve

Dave   Julie   Harry

Diana

LISTENING

1 Look at the different dances in the photos. Where do you think they come from? Choose from the countries in the list.

Brazil | China | Greece | Indonesia
Spain | Thailand | Turkey

2 In which photos can you see these things? Write 1–4 in the boxes.

1 A man is playing a guitar and a woman is dancing.
2 The men are wearing clothes of different colours.
3 The men and the women are dancing in a line.
4 The men are wearing black-and-white cloths round their legs.

3 ◀))2.14 Listen to the programme. Which three photos in Exercise 1 do the people talk about?

4 ◀))2.14 Listen again and choose the correct options.

0 Janie's family goes to (Spain)/ Turkey every year.
1 Janie loves the clothes that the men / women wear.
2 The dancers in Turkey wear skirts that are the same colour / different colours.
3 The dancers in Turkey don't have any music / stop.
4 In the Kecak dance, there isn't any music / moving.
5 The Kecak dance is only for tourists / musicians.

5 Imagine you can go and watch one of the dances. Which dance do you want to watch?

FUNCTIONS
Describing a scene

1 Match 1–3 with a–c.
When we describe a scene, we often use:

1 the present continuous
2 prepositions
3 adjectives

a for colours, sizes, etc.
b to say what people are doing.
c to say where people and things are.

2 Read the text and answer the questions.

1 Which photo in Listening Exercise 1 is this person describing?
2 Underline examples of the language mentioned in Exercise 1 (present continuous, prepositions, adjectives).

> There are lots of people. One woman is dancing. She's wearing a red dress. There are some musicians behind her. They're playing music. Some people are sitting on chairs. They are watching and clapping. Everyone is happy. They're enjoying the music and dancing.

3 **SPEAKING** Look at the picture. Work in pairs. Describe the scene.

READING

1 🔊 **2.15** Read and listen to the dialogue and look at the picture. Who is Andy?

MAGGIE	Hi, Mike. Are you enjoying the party?
MIKE	Hey, Maggie. Yeah, it's OK. But I don't like the music.
MAGGIE	Oh, the music is OK! Hey! Come and dance! I really like dancing!
MIKE	No, thanks. I don't like dancing very much. Ask Andy to dance with you. He's a really good dancer.
MAGGIE	Andy? Who's Andy?
MIKE	He's over there. Look – he's wearing grey trousers and a green shirt. Can you see him?
MAGGIE	Oh, yes, I can see him. A green shirt!! Ugh!
MIKE	Oh, it's just a shirt! Go and ask him to dance.
MAGGIE	No. I hate talking to boys.
MIKE	But you're talking to *me*.
MAGGIE	I know, but you're my friend. That's different. I don't know Andy. *And* he's wearing a green shirt!
MIKE	You're crazy. Andy is really nice. He loves going to parties, and dancing … and meeting new people. Oh, look, he's coming over here.
ANDY	Hi. I'm Andy.
MAGGIE	Oh, hi. I'm Maggie. Do you like dancing?
ANDY	Yes, I love it! Do you want to dance?
MAGGIE	Yes, OK! Oh, and I like your shirt!
MIKE	What? Wow. I really don't understand!

2 Read the dialogue again and complete the sentences.

0 Mike is enjoying the party but _he doesn't like the music_ .

1 Andy is wearing

_____ .

2 Maggie doesn't like

_____ .

3 Maggie and Mike are

_____ .

GRAMMAR

like / don't like + -ing

1 Complete the sentences from the dialogue in Reading Exercise 1. Then complete the rule.

0 Come and dance! I really like _dancing_ !

1 I hate _____ to boys.

2 He loves _____ to parties.

3 Do you like _____ ?

> **RULE:** We use the verbs (*don't*) *like* / ¹_____ / *hate* + verb + *-ing* to talk about activities.

2 Write *like*, *don't like*, *love* and *hate* in the correct places.

😊😊 **1** _____

😊 **2** _____

☹ **3** _____

☹☹ **4** _____

3 Complete the sentences. Use a verb from Exercise 2 and the correct form of the verb in brackets.

0 I _love watching_ sport on TV. 😊 😊 (watch)

1 I _____ to the cinema. ☹ (go)

2 I _____ early. ☹ ☹ (get up)

3 My family _____ to France on holiday. 😊 (go)

4 My best friend _____ . 😊 😊 (run)

5 My parents _____ . ☹ (dance)

6 _____ your parents _____? 😊 (cook)

7 _____ the teacher _____ homework? 😊 (give)

4 Look at sentences 0–5 in Exercise 3. Which are true for you? Change the ones that are not true for you.

Workbook page 73 ▶

VOCABULARY
Clothes

1 🔊 2.16 **Match the clothes in the list with the pictures. Write 1–12 in the boxes. Listen and check.**

1 a dress | 2 a coat | 3 jeans | 4 a jumper
5 a shirt | 6 shoes | 7 shorts | 8 a skirt
9 socks | 10 a T-shirt | 11 trainers | 12 trousers

Paul

Anna

Jason

Amanda

Simon

2 **Look at the pictures in Exercise 1 again. What are the people wearing?**

0 Paul is wearing
   blue jeans, a white T-shirt and trainers .
1 Anna is wearing _____ .
2 Jason _____ .
3 Amanda _____ .
4 Simon _____ .

3 **SPEAKING** **Work in pairs. Ask and answer the questions.**

1 What clothes do you love wearing? What clothes do you hate wearing?
2 Do you like shopping for clothes? Why? / Why not?
3 What is your teacher wearing today?
4 Which colour do you love or hate wearing?

> I love wearing jeans and trainers but I hate wearing shoes and trousers.

Workbook page 75

Pronunciation
Intonation – listing items
Go to page 121. 🔊

▮TRAIN TO THiNK ▮
Memorising

1 Look at the picture for two minutes.

2 **SPEAKING** Student A: Turn to page 127. Student B: Turn to page 128. Listen to the questions your partner asks and answer with short answers. Correct the negative answers.

Culture

Musical instruments around the world

1

The berimbau

A

This is a Brazilian instrument. It's made of wood. It's long and thin and has got one string. You play the berimbau by hitting the string with a stick. Musicians play the berimbau when people dance capoeira. Capoeira is now famous in many parts of the world, not only in Brazil.

Brazil

2

The didgeridoo

B

The didgeridoo is a famous musical instrument that comes from Australia. It's like a big, long trumpet, but it's made of wood. You blow into it, and it makes a very unusual deep sound. Didgeridoos are difficult to hold because they are between one and three metres long. The musician usually puts the didgeridoo on the ground.

Australia

3

The bonang

C

The bonang is a group of round, metal pots. Musicians play these in Indonesia, in an orchestra of many musicians. You put the pots together in lines. You then hit the pots with a stick that has a piece of cloth around it. All the pots are different sizes and so they all make different sounds. Some people say that the sound is very relaxing.

Indonesia

1 Look at the photos on page 80. Find these five things and one action.

a piece of cloth | a stick
an orchestra | blow (verb)
the ground | wood

2 Read and listen to the article. Which countries do the musical instruments come from?

3 Read the article again. Mark the sentences T (true) or F (false).

0	There is only one string on a berimbau.	T
1	Capoeira is the music that you play on the berimbau.	
2	A didgeridoo is like a trumpet.	
3	Didgeridoos are always the same size.	
4	The bonang has got one pot.	
5	You play the bonang using a stick.	

4 **SPEAKING** Are there any special musical instruments in your country? Can you play any musical instruments? Tell the class.

WRITING
Describing a scene

1 Read these three Tweets and look at the photos. Where is Sandy? Tick the correct photo.

2 Read the Tweets again. Underline examples of the present continuous.

3 Write notes to describe how you are feeling in each of these situations.

1 You're at a bus stop. It's raining. You're going to meet friends to see a local band play. The bus doesn't come.
2 You're at home. You have to study. The weather outside is very nice and you want to go out but you have to stay inside.
3 You're at home. You're watching a great film. You want to tell your friends that it's really good.

4 Write three Tweets for each situation in Exercise 3.

Remember:
• A Tweet can only be 140 characters (including spaces).
• You can say something in your second and third Tweet about how the situation is changing.

3.22
Here we are. We're waiting. I think there are more than 3,000 people here! It's fantastic. People are singing and smiling – great!

3.28
I think they're coming out now. Yes – here they are! Everyone is shouting and cheering!! And the band are smiling. They're very happy.

3.49
They're playing my favourite song! I'm so happy and my friends are smiling and singing. I'm watching my favourite band – this is the best!

LISTENING
Part 1: Multiple-choice pictures

1 🔊2.20 **You will hear five short conversations. There is one question for each conversation.**
For each question choose the right answer (A, B or C).

0   What time does Bob get home from school?

A ☐   B ✓   C ☐

1   When is Sue's birthday?

A ☐   B ☐   C ☐

2   What is Lucy's favourite month?

A ☐   B ☐   C ☐

3   Which instrument does Mike play?

A ☐   B ☐   C ☐

4   Which of Jenny's clothes does Liam like?

A ☐   B ☐   C ☐

READING AND WRITING
Part 6: Word completion

2   **Read the descriptions of some words about sport. What is the word for each one? The first letter is already there. There is one space for each other letter in the word.**

0   You need a bike to do this.

   c y c l e

1   You do this in white clothes.

   t _ _ _ k _ _ _ _ _ _

2   You need snow to do this.

   s _ _ _ _ _ _ _ _

3   You play this in a team of six people.

   v _ _ _ _ _ _ _ _ _ _

4   You do this in the sea.

   s _ _ _

5   In this sport you throw a ball through a hoop.

   b _ _ _ _ _ _ _ _ _

VOCABULARY

1 Complete the sentences with the words in the list. There are two extra words.

cheering | coat | doing | making | rugby | sitting
studying | surf | taking | third | three | trainers

1 It's cold outside. Put a _____ on when you go out.
2 I love playing _____ .
3 We like _____ in the garden on hot summer days.
4 I'm in the kitchen. I'm _____ sandwiches for the party.
5 My brother is in Australia. He's _____ English at a university there.
6 You can't wear _____ to a party! Wear your new shoes!
7 My sister's at the sports centre. She's _____ tae kwon do.
8 I love _____ photos of different sports.
9 My birthday? It's on the _____ of December.
10 They're winning! Everyone is _____ !

/10

GRAMMAR

2 Complete the sentences with the words in the box.

can | can't | don't | like | stand | standing

1 Do you _____ reading magazines?
2 I don't like _____ on the bus.
3 I'm ill. I _____ go out today.
4 I don't want to sit down. I can _____ and watch. It's OK.
5 We really _____ like going for walks in winter.
6 He _____ run 100 metres in twelve seconds.

3 Find and correct the mistake in each sentence.

1 He can to count to twenty in German.
2 Please be quiet. I'm study for the test tomorrow.
3 She doesn't can speak English.
4 I don't like watch sport.
5 She's in town right now. She shops.
6 Do you can play the piano?

/12

FUNCTIONAL LANGUAGE

4 Write the missing words.

1 A _____ the time?
   B It's three _____ . I'm bored!
   A Me too. Why _____ we play a game?
   B A game? No thanks. _____ about going for a walk?
2 A Look at those people! They're _____ very strange clothes.
   B Yes, they're going to a big party in the park. It's a holiday today!
   A What _____ does the party start?
   B At two o'clock. Oh, look! It's quarter _____ two now!
      _____ go and join them.

/8

MY SCORE /30

| 22 – 30 |
| 10 – 21 |
| 0 – 9 |

READING

1 **Look at the photos. Where can you see the words in the list? Write 1–8 in the boxes.**

  1 a carrot cake | 2 a chef
  3 a plate | 4 cooking
  5 an omelette | 6 tomato soup
  7 some salad | 8 steak

2 **SPEAKING** **What other food words do you know?**

  pizza, apples, hamburgers, …

3 **SPEAKING** **Tell your partner what food you like and don't like.**

  I like … I don't like …

4 **Look at the photos on page 85. What is unusual about the chefs? Read and check.**

5 🔊 2.21 **Read and listen to the article. Mark the sentences T (true), F (false) or DS (doesn't say).**

  0 Harry is ten years old and he's from New York. — T
  1 He wants to be a star chef.
  2 His sister likes cooking too, but she's not very good.
  3 The other children on the TV show aren't very good cooks.
  4 Children must be ten years old to be on *Star Junior Chefs*.
  5 The chefs' hands must be clean.
  6 It's OK for the children to eat the food they are cooking.
  7 After the TV show Harry goes home to study.

Young kitchen stars

Harry doesn't want to be a star chef when he's 20. He wants to be one now. This is why he's on the *Star Junior Chefs* TV programme.

The ten-year-old New Yorker likes cooking. He can make fantastic soups and salads, excellent omelettes and the best cakes. But there are many other children on the show, too. And they are all very good.

More and more young people are interested in cooking. Many of them learn it from their parents. Others watch special cooking videos for children on YouTube©. In many cities, there are special cooking classes for young people. Some of them are for children from the age of three!

But what must you do to become a star chef? Of course, it's important that you like cooking and are really good at it. But there are some rules. You must be nine years old or more to be on *Star Junior Chefs*. 'We must wash our hands before we start cooking,' Harry says. 'And of course we mustn't put them in our mouths. A chef doesn't do that! And we must be very careful with hot plates.'

The show starts. Harry is excited. He knows he's an excellent cook. This time he makes tomato soup, some salad, steak and carrot cake. The experts in the studio love Harry's food, and he stays on the show.

It's 5 pm. The show is over. Harry is happy, and a little tired. He goes home. It's time to do his homework.

■ THiNK VALUES ■

How you eat is important

1 **SPEAKING** How often do you do these things? Write *always*, *sometimes*, *often* or *never*. Then tell the class.

☐	a	sit at a table to eat _____
☐	b	eat alone _____
☐	c	eat slowly _____
☐	d	eat very fast _____
☐	e	eat with other people _____
☐	f	eat and play computer games at the same time _____

I always eat slowly. I sometimes eat with other people.

2 Look again at the things in Exercise 1. Are they good things to do? Write 1–3 in the boxes: 1 = a good thing to do, 2 = an OK thing to do, 3 = a bad thing to do.

3 **SPEAKING** Compare your ideas with a partner.

I often eat …

I think … is good.

I think … is not so good.

GRAMMAR
must / mustn't

1 Complete the sentences from the article on page 85 with *must* or *mustn't*. Then complete the rule.

1 You _____ be nine years old or more to be on *Star Junior Chefs*.

2 We _____ wash our hands before we start cooking.

3 We _____ put them in our mouths.

> **RULE:** We use *must* and *mustn't* to talk about rules.
> Use ¹_____ to say that it's necessary to do something.
> Use ²_____ to say that it's not OK to do something.

2 Complete the dialogues. Use *must* or *mustn't* and a verb from the list.

buy | eat | forget | ~~give~~

0 A Hey, can I borrow this book?
  B Sure, but you _*must give*_ it back next week.

1 A Mum, can I have some chocolate?
  B Of course not! You know you _____ chocolate before lunch.

2 A It's Julia's birthday next week.
  B That's right. We _____ to buy her a present.

3 A Oh, no. There isn't any milk.
  B I _____ some after work.

3 **SPEAKING** Work in pairs. Think of some things that are important for you to do (or not do) in the next few days.

> I must write an email to my friend Mark.

> I mustn't forget to clean my room.

Workbook page 82

VOCABULARY
Food and drink

1 🔊 2.22 Write the names of the food and drink under the photos. Listen and check.

2 **SPEAKING** Which word in each group is different? Why?

1 coffee – potato – tea
2 banana – orange – burger
3 carrot – chicken – beef
4 milk – strawberry – apple
5 pepper – potato – lamb

> Number 1 is potato – coffee and tea are drinks.

3 **SPEAKING** Look at the food words in Exercise 1. Work in pairs. Ask and answer questions to find three things you both like.

> Do you like tomatoes?

> Yes, I love them. And you?

> I like them. Do you like ...?

Workbook page 85

Meat

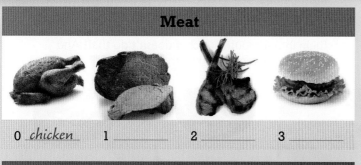

0 *chicken*   1 _____   2 _____   3 _____

Fruit

4 _____   5 _____   6 _____   7 _____

Vegetables

8 _____   9 _____   10 _____   11 _____

Drinks

12 _____   13 _____   14 _____   15 _____

LISTENING

1 **Look at the picture. What's happening?**

2 ◀)2.23 **Listen to the dialogue. What is George cooking? Does he eat it?**

3 ◀)2.23 **Listen again. Put the sentences in the order you hear them. Write 1–6 in the boxes.**

	a	Can I clean the kitchen later?
1	b	Can I make an omelette?
	c	Can I come into the kitchen now?
	d	I must be quick now.
	e	Would you like some help?
	f	Can I go to the pizza place?

GRAMMAR
can (asking for permission)

1 **Match these answers to the questions in Listening Exercise 3. Then read the rule.**

1 OK, but don't forget to do it. ☐

2 Yes, you can. ☐

3 No, wait, Mum. ☐

> **RULE:** We use *can* + subject to ask if it's OK to do something.

2 ◀)2.24 **Complete the questions with *can* and a verb from the list. Listen and check.**

~~do~~ | eat | go out | play | try on | use

0 <u>*Can*</u> I <u>*do*</u> my homework later, please?

1 _____ I _____ these jeans, please?

2 _____ I _____ your laptop, please?

3 Dad, _____ I _____ tonight?

4 _____ we _____ football in the garden?

5 _____ we _____ dinner in front of the TV?

3 **Match the answers with the questions in Exercise 2.**

0	a	No, you can't. Do it now.
	b	Of course you can. But be careful.
	c	No you can't, you've got school tomorrow.
	d	Sorry, I need it to write some emails.
	e	Yes, the changing room is over there.
	f	Well, OK … , it's your birthday.

Workbook page 82 ▶

■ THiNK SELF-ESTEEM ■
You are what you eat

1 **Think about what is true for you. Circle 1–5: 1 = certainly true, 5 = certainly not true.**

1	I often eat between meals.	1 – 2 – 3 – 4 – 5
2	I always eat breakfast.	1 – 2 – 3 – 4 – 5
3	I eat fruit and vegetables every day.	1 – 2 – 3 – 4 – 5
4	I drink lots of water.	1 – 2 – 3 – 4 – 5
5	I eat lots of sweets.	1 – 2 – 3 – 4 – 5
6	I brush my teeth after every meal.	1 – 2 – 3 – 4 – 5

2 **SPEAKING** **Compare your answers with a partner.**

> I often eat between meals.

> I eat fruit every day.

READING

1 Read the menu. What would you choose to eat?

2 🔊 2.25 Read and listen to the dialogue. What doesn't Jack like?

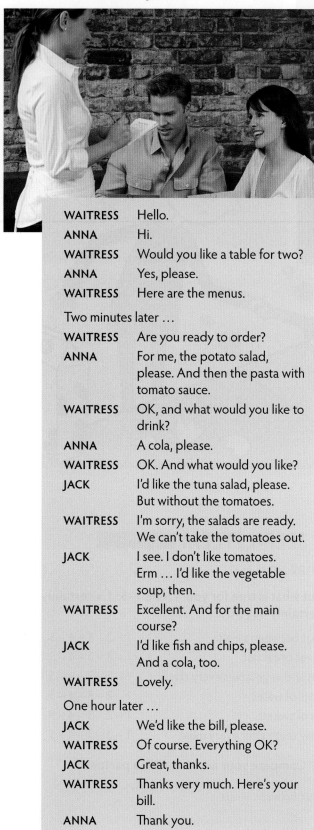

WAITRESS	Hello.
ANNA	Hi.
WAITRESS	Would you like a table for two?
ANNA	Yes, please.
WAITRESS	Here are the menus.

Two minutes later …

WAITRESS	Are you ready to order?
ANNA	For me, the potato salad, please. And then the pasta with tomato sauce.
WAITRESS	OK, and what would you like to drink?
ANNA	A cola, please.
WAITRESS	OK. And what would you like?
JACK	I'd like the tuna salad, please. But without the tomatoes.
WAITRESS	I'm sorry, the salads are ready. We can't take the tomatoes out.
JACK	I see. I don't like tomatoes. Erm … I'd like the vegetable soup, then.
WAITRESS	Excellent. And for the main course?
JACK	I'd like fish and chips, please. And a cola, too.
WAITRESS	Lovely.

One hour later …

JACK	We'd like the bill, please.
WAITRESS	Of course. Everything OK?
JACK	Great, thanks.
WAITRESS	Thanks very much. Here's your bill.
ANNA	Thank you.

3 Read the dialogue again. What does Anna eat? What does Jack eat?

Zoe's café

Menu

Our starters

Potato salad	£5.25
Salad (tuna fish and tomato)	£7.50
Vegetable soup	£6.60

Our main courses

Steak	£15.80
Pasta with tomato sauce	£8.50
Fish and chips	£8.50
Hamburger and chips	£7.80
Chicken and tomato sandwich	£6.50
Jacket potato	£5.20

Our desserts

Ice cream (per scoop)	£1.20
Vanilla, strawberry, lemon and chocolate	

Our drinks

Fruit juice (orange or apple)	£1.90
Cola	£1.70
Coffee	£2.20
Tea	£1.60
Water	£1.10

4 Who says these things in a restaurant? Write W (waiter/waitress) or C (customer) in the boxes.

0	Can I help you?	W
1	A table for two, please.	
2	Here are the menus.	
3	Are you ready to order?	
4	What would you like to drink?	
5	I'd like the vegetable soup, then.	
6	Can we have the bill, please?	
7	Would you like dessert?	

GRAMMAR
I'd like … / Would you like …?

1 Complete these sentences from the dialogue on page 88. Then complete the rule.

1 Would you _____ a table for two?

2 _____ like the vegetable soup, then.

3 What _____ you like to drink?

4 _____ like the bill, please.

> **RULE:** We use *I* + *would* (*'d*) + ¹_____ to ask for something in a nice way.
> We use *Would* + *you* + ²_____ ? to offer something.

2 How do you say *I'd like …* and *Would you like …?* in your language?

3 Put the words in the correct order to make sentences or questions.

0 like / a / I'd / please / banana .
  I'd like a banana, please.

1 like / some / you / would / coffee ?

2 like / fish / I'd / and / please / chips ,

3 you / what / to / would / like / eat ?

4 to / we'd / like / here / sit .

5 would / this afternoon / what / you / like / to / do ?

4 Complete what the people are saying.

1 _____ to order now?

2 _____ some coffee?

3 We _____ to sit there, please.

4 I _____, some ice cream, please.

5 **SPEAKING** Work in groups. One of you is the waiter at Zoe's café, the others order food and drinks. Act out the situation.

> Workbook page 83

> ### Pronunciation
> Intonation – giving two choices
> **Go to page 121.**

VOCABULARY
Meals

1 ◀))2.28 Match the words in the list to the items in the picture. Write 1–9 in the boxes. Listen and check.

1 bread | 2 butter | 3 cereal | 4 egg | 5 fruit
6 honey | 7 jam | 8 toast | 9 yoghurt

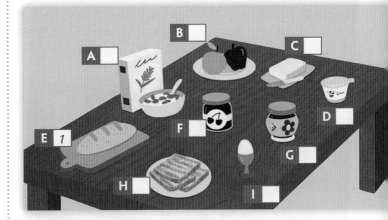

2 **SPEAKING** Copy the table into your notebook and complete it. Then tell the class.

	always	often	sometimes	never
breakfast				
lunch				
dinner				

> *For breakfast I always drink …*

> *I never have (any) … for lunch.*

> Workbook page 85

WRITING
A meal plan for your friend

1 Ask a partner to give you his/her table from Vocabulary Exercise 2. Imagine he/she is staying at your home for the weekend. You want to make meals that he/she likes. Write a menu for him/her.

2 Show your ideas to your partner. Is he/she happy with the meals?

Saturday   *Sunday*

Breakfast: *Breakfast:*

Lunch: *Lunch:*

Dinner: *Dinner:*

The pizza

1 **Look at the photos and answer the questions.**

Who can you see in the photos?
Where are they and what are they doing?

2 🔊2.29 **Now read and listen to the photostory. What does Ruby hate?**

DAD So what are you doing, boys?
DAN Tom is making pizza for the girls, and I'm helping him.
TOM Is that OK, Dad?
DAD Of course. No problem. You make great pizza! What time do they get here?
TOM Six o'clock. We've got half an hour.

1

DAD Do you want some help, Tom?
TOM No, I'm OK, thanks. OK, first we need to add the tomato sauce.
DAN Can I cut the peppers for you?
TOM OK.
DAD Just be careful with the knife.

2

TOM What are you doing, Dad?
DAD I'm putting a bit of cheese on the pizza.
DAN Don't do that!
DAD Too late.

3

DAD It's only cheese.
DAN The thing is, Ruby hates cheese.
DAD She hates cheese? Oh, dear.
TOM Now what?
DAD We can't make another one. We haven't got time.
TOM What can we do?

4

DEVELOPING SPEAKING

3 ◼️◀ EP5 **Watch to find out how the story continues.**

1 Who does Tom's dad call?

2 Why are the boys surprised?

4 ◼️◀ EP5 **Watch again. Put the events in order. Write 1–6 in the boxes.**

☐	a	The man from Andy's Chicken House arrives.
☐	b	The girls eat the pizza.
☐	c	They all wait in the hall.
1	d	Tom's dad calls Andy's Chicken House.
☐	e	The girls arrive.
☐	f	The girls say hello to Tom's dad.

PHRASES FOR FLUENCY

1 **Find the expressions 1–4 in the story. Who says them?**

1 Of course.

2 be careful …

3 a bit (of) …

4 The thing is, …

2 **How do you say the expressions in Exercise 1 in your language?**

3 **Put the sentences in the correct order to make a dialogue.**

☐	GREG	Well, the thing is, I want to cook some Italian food.
1	GREG	Do you like Italian food?
☐	GREG	That's right. I don't know how to cook very well.
☐	NADIA	Oh. And you need a bit of help.
☐	NADIA	Of course. I love spaghetti and stuff. Why?
☐	NADIA	OK. You can use my mum's cookbook. But be careful! She loves that book!

4 **Complete the dialogues with the expressions from Exercise 1.**

1 A Let's go to the cinema tonight.

 B No thanks. I've got ___*a bit of*___ work to do.

 A Really? On Saturday?

 B No, not really. I'm sorry. _____, I haven't got any money.

2 A Can I look at your new phone?

 B _____ . Here it is.

 A Oh, it's really nice!

 B Thanks, I love it. Oh, _____ ! Don't break it!

FUNCTIONS
Offering and asking for help

1 **Look at the photostory again. Who says these expressions?**

1 Can I cut the peppers for you?

2 Do you want some help?

2 **Match the possible answers to questions 1 and 2 in Exercise 1.**

a	OK.	1
b	Yes, please.	☐
c	Sure, thanks.	☐
d	No, I'm OK, thanks.	☐

3 **Work in pairs. Write a short dialogue for each picture. Use expressions from Exercises 1 and 2.**

4 **SPEAKING** **Act out your dialogues.**

READING

1 Match the words in the list with the photos. Write 1–6 in the boxes.

1 achievements | 2 astronaut | 3 factory
4 sky diving | 5 spacecraft | 6 stamps

2 Look at the photos and answer the questions.

1 What are the names of the two people?
2 Where were they from?
3 Why are they famous?

3 Name some famous people in your country. Why are they famous?

4 ◀)2.30 Read and listen to the article and answer the question.

Why is Valentina Tereshkova famous?

5 Read the article again and put the events in order.

- [ ] **a** Tereshkova was in space for three days.
- [ ] **b** She was named 'Woman of the Century'.
- [ ] **c** She was the carrier of the Olympic flag.
- [ ] **d** There was a competition to find new astronauts.
- [1] **e** Valentina Tereshkova was born.

A

B 1

C

D

E

F

It was her dream to be an astronaut

Valentina Tereshkova was born in Russia on 6th March, 1937. Her father was a driver and her mother was a factory worker. Valentina was a worker in a factory, too. Her hobby was sky diving and it was her dream to be an astronaut and to go into space.

In 1962, there was a big competition to find new astronauts. There were 400 people interested in going to space. The training programme wasn't very easy, but Tereshkova was hard working. She was the lucky one. Tereshkova's big day was 16th June, 1963, and she was ready.

The name of her spacecraft was Vostok 6, and Tereshkova was the first woman in space. The flight was very difficult because there were many technical problems and Tereshkova wasn't very well for most of the flight. She was in space for three days. She is the only woman to do a solo space flight. After that she was very famous all over the world. Her face was on stamps in several countries.

In the year 2000, there was a big celebration in London and Valentina Tereshkova was named the 'Woman of the Century'.

At the opening ceremony of the Winter Olympics in Russia in 2014, Valentina Tereshkova was one of the carriers of the Olympic flag.

These moments were very important to her.

THiNK VALUES
Hard work and achievement

1 In 2000, Valentina Tereshkova was named 'Woman of the Century'. Which of the following, do you think, were important for her success? Write N (not important) or I (important).

1 She was born in 1937.

2 Her father was a driver.

3 She was a factory worker.

4 It was her dream to be an astronaut and go into space.

5 She was hard working in the training programme.

6 She was lucky.

7 The flight was difficult, but Tereshkova was strong.

8 She was in space for three days.

2 **SPEAKING** Compare your answers with a partner. Do you agree?

> She was born in 1937. I think that was important for her success because it was the start of space travel.

> I agree. / I don't agree. I think …

GRAMMAR

Past simple: was / wasn't; were / weren't; there was / were

1 **Complete the sentences from the text on page 93. Then complete the rule and the table.**

1 Valentina Tereshkova _____ born on 6th March, 1937

2 The training programme _____ very easy.

3 There _____ 400 people interested in going to space.

4 These moments _____ very important to her.

RULE: was/were is the past form of [1] _____ .

Positive	Negative
I/he/she/it [1]_____	I/he/she/it **wasn't (was not)**
We/you/they **were**	We/you/they [3]_____ (**were not**)
There **was** / [2]_____	There [4]_____ / **weren't**

2 **Complete the sentences with was, wasn't, were or weren't.**

1 My friends and I ___were___ at the shopping centre yesterday. My sister _____ there too, but my parents _____ because they _____ at work.

2 There _____ lots of people in the shopping centre. There _____ a little girl with her dog. The dog _____ very nice. Its name _____ Blackie.

Workbook page 90

VOCABULARY

Time expressions: past

1 🔊2.31 **Write in, at, last and yesterday to complete the time expressions. Listen and check.**

1 _____ weekend / Sunday / night / week / month / year

2 _____ morning / afternoon / evening

3 _____ 2014

4 _____ four o'clock / 5.30 / 6 am / 6 pm

2 **Look at the pictures. Write sentences to say where the people were and when. Use in, at, last or yesterday.**

at the cinema | in Paris | at the football match
at a birthday party | at the park | at her grandparents'
Lillian was at the park at quarter past eleven, yesterday morning.

3 **Make notes about where you were yesterday at the times in the pictures A, C and E in Exercise 2.**

4 **SPEAKING Work in pairs. Tell your partner where you were yesterday. Find out about your partner.**

> I was at home at quarter past eleven, yesterday morning. What about you?

> I was at my cousin's house.

5 **SPEAKING Use the information about your partner to report to the class.**

> Yesterday morning, Maria was at home. At half past three yesterday afternoon, she was at a friend's house. In the evening, she was at her grandma's house. She was at the cinema with her mum at nine o'clock, last night.

A Lillian
B Joseph
C Leo
D July 2014 Sam
E Camilla
F Evelyn

Workbook page 93

LISTENING

1 Look at the picture. Where was Freddie on Saturday evening? Where was Vicky? Use ideas from the box to help you.

> On Saturday evening, Freddie was …
> He was … There were …
> The band were …
> The music was …
>
> Vicky was …
> She was … There were …
> The film was …
> The actors were …

2 🔊 2.32 Listen to the dialogue and check your answers.

3 🔊 2.32 Listen again and match the questions with the answers.

0	Does Freddie say it was a good party?	e
1	Were there a lot of people?	
2	Who were the five boys at the party?	
3	What was the name of the band?	
4	Were One Direction at the party?	
5	How was the music for Freddie?	

a No, there weren't.
b One Direction.
c It wasn't bad.
d They were from a band.
e Yes, he says it was fantastic.
f No, they weren't, but their music was.

GRAMMAR

Past simple: *Was he …? / Were you …?*

1 Put the words in the correct order to make questions.

1 you / the cinema / were / at / ?
2 the music / good / was / ?
3 a lot of / people / were / there / ?

2 Match the answers below with the questions in Exercise 1. Then complete the table.

a	Yes, it was.
b	No, there weren't.
c	No, I wasn't.

Question	Short answer
Was I/he/she/it … ? ¹_____ we/you/ they … ?	Yes, I/he/she **was**. No, I/he/she ²_____. Yes, we/you/they ³_____. No, we/you/they **weren't**.

3 🔊 2.33 Complete the dialogue with *was*, *were*, *wasn't* or *weren't*. Then listen and check.

JENNY   Oh, no!

PEDRO   What's the matter?

JENNY   My phone? Where is it? It ⁰ ___was___ in my jacket!

PEDRO   OK, calm down. Where ¹_____ your phone this morning?

JENNY   Well, I ²_____ at home from nine o'clock to ten o'clock.

PEDRO   And then? ³_____ you in town?

JENNY   Yes, I ⁴_____. I ⁵_____ in the shopping centre. And I'm 100% sure that my phone ⁶_____ in my pocket.

PEDRO   ⁷_____ Steve and Maisie with you?

JENNY   No, they ⁸_____. I ⁹_____ in the shoe shop. I bought some new shoes.

PEDRO   Wait a minute. Let me call you.

JENNY   It's ringing! Oh, look! It's in the shoe bag! It ¹⁰_____ there all the time!

Workbook page 90

FUNCTIONS

Asking for information about the past

1 Write *was* or *were* to complete the questions. Then ask and answer the questions with a partner. Check your answers on page 93.

1 _____ Valentina Tereshkova born in Russia?
2 _____ her parents astronauts, too?
3 _____ there 400 people interested in the competition?
4 _____ the flight very easy or very difficult?
5 _____ the Winter Olympics in Russia in 2013?

2 Make notes to answer the following questions.

1 Where were you at 3 pm on Saturday?
2 What was your hobby when you were eight?
3 How old were you in May 2014?
4 How old was your best friend last year?

3 **SPEAKING** Work in pairs. Ask and answer the questions in Exercise 2.

READING

1 Look at the pictures of two film heroes. What do you know about them? What special powers have they got?

> I think Storm can ...

> Maybe Percy is ...

2 🔊 2.34 Read and listen to the article and check your answers.

Fictional heroes

Who is she? Storm

What's her story?

Storm's story started in New York, where she was born. Her mum was a princess and her dad worked as a photographer. When Storm was six, she moved to Cairo, Egypt with her parents. One day a plane crashed into their house. Storm's parents died, and she was alone in the big city. Her life in Cairo was very hard. When she was a teenager, Storm discovered that she had special powers, and she started to use them – not always successfully.

What are her powers?

Storm has control over the weather. She can change the temperature. She can make rain, sunshine, hurricanes, clouds and storms.

Who is he? Percy Jackson

What's his story?

His father is Poseidon, the Greek god of the sea. His half-brother is called Tyson. Tyson is a monster. At first, Percy hated his monster brother. Later, Percy and Tyson tried to help each other in their many adventures. In the end, they were friends. Percy was never afraid and he never worried about his life. He helped the people he liked.

What are his powers?

Percy is very strong because he is the son of the god of the sea. He's a very fast swimmer. He can stay underwater for a long time. He can talk to sea animals and he can make sea storms.

3 Read the article again. Mark the sentences T (true) or F (false).

0	Storm was born in a city in the USA.	T
1	Storm's parents died in a city in the USA.	☐
2	As a little girl, Storm lived a very difficult life.	☐
3	Storm was good at using her special powers at the beginning.	☐
4	Percy's father was the god of the hurricanes.	☐
5	Percy's brother was a monster.	☐
6	Percy and Tyson were not friends at the beginning.	☐

▣ TRAIN TO THiNK ▣

Sequencing

1 Put the sentences in order to tell Kidhero's story.

☐	a	There was a very fast car on the road.
8	b	Kidhero was very happy.
☐	c	There were also two young children in the road.
1	d	It was a hot day and Kidhero wanted an ice cream.
☐	e	He walked to an ice cream shop.
☐	f	Kidhero jumped in front of the car and stopped it with his hand.
☐	g	He saved the children.
☐	h	He walked out of the shop with his ice cream.

2 **SPEAKING** Work in pairs. Tell the story. Can you include these lines?

He walked back home.

Kidhero started to run.

The children smiled.

GRAMMAR
Past simple: regular verbs

1 Write the base form of the verbs.

Base form	0 *help*	1	2	3
Past simple	helped	started	moved	tried

2 Complete the sentences from the text on page 96 with the past forms from Exercise 1. Then complete the rule.

1 Storm's story _____ in New York.

2 When Storm was six, she _____ to Cairo.

3 Percy and Tyson _____ to help each other.

4 He _____ the people he liked.

> **RULE:** To form the past simple of regular verbs, add
> ¹_____ to the base form.
>
> When the verb ends in -e, add -d.
>
> When the verb ends in consonant + -y, change y to
> ²_____ and add -ed.

3 Write the past simple forms of these verbs. Check your answers in the text on page 96.

1 work 4 crash

2 die 5 like

3 hate 6 worry

4 Complete the text about Bruce Wayne. Use the past simple form of the verbs in brackets.

SUPER heroes

Bruce Wayne is Batman. When Bruce Wayne was a child, he and his parents were in the streets of Gotham City and a man ⁰ ___*attacked*___ (attack) them. The man ¹_____ (kill) Bruce's parents. The police ²_____ (arrive) too late. After this, Bruce ³_____ (decide) to fight crime.

For many years, Bruce ⁴_____ (work) hard to become a crime fighter. He ⁵_____ (call) himself 'Batman', and ⁶_____ (try) hard to fight the bad people in Gotham. His best friend was James Gordon, a police officer. He had other friends, too. They all ⁷_____ (help) him to fight the criminals of Gotham.

Workbook page 91

Pronunciation
Past simple regular verbs
Go to page 121.

VOCABULARY
The weather

1 ◀)) 2.37 Match the sentences in the list with the pictures. Write 1–8 in the boxes. Listen and check.

1 It's raining. | 2 It's sunny. | 3 It's windy.
4 It's cloudy. | 5 It's snowing. | 6 It's hot.
7 It's cold. | 8 It's warm.

2 Complete the dialogues with some of the phrases from Exercise 1. Sometimes there is more than one correct answer.

0 A What's the weather like?

B ___*It's raining.*___ Take an umbrella.

1 A Bye, Mum.

B Bye. But you don't need a jumper. _____ outside.

2 A Hey look! _____ !

B Great! We can go skiing later!

3 A Wow, _____ today.

B I know! You must hold on to your hat!

3 **SPEAKING** Work in pairs. Write similar dialogues and act them out.

Workbook page 93

Culture

Statues

There are many strange and wonderful statues all over the world.

Charles La Trobe was an important man in Melbourne, Australia in the 1800s. He improved the city for people. For example, he created a lot of parks. These days in Melbourne there are lots of things to remember him. There's a La Trobe University and a La Trobe Street. There's a statue of him at the University – upside down!

Franz Kafka was a writer from Prague. He was born in 1883. His books were in German. During his life he was not very famous but now he is. Many of his stories were very strange. There's a very unusual statue of him in Prague. He's sitting on the shoulders of an empty suit!

Hidesaburō Ueno was a professor at Tokyo University. Every day he travelled to work by train. When he arrived home in the evening, his dog, Hachiko was always at the station to meet him. One day Mr Ueno died. He never arrived home again. For eight more years Hachiko waited at the station every day. When Hachiko died, they made a statue of him. You can see it at the station.

In the middle of the Atacama Desert in Chile a big hand comes out of the sand. It's 70 kilometres from the nearest town. *Mano de Desierto* (The Hand of the Desert) is 11 metres tall and is the work of the Chilean sculptor Mario Irarrázabal.

1 Look at the photos on page 98. Find these things.

desert | sand | shoulders
suit | upside down

2 ◀》2.38 Read and listen to the article. Where are the statues?

3 Read the article again. Mark the sentences T (true) or F (false).

0	Charles La Trobe helped the people of Melbourne.	T
1	Franz Kafka was from Germany.	
2	Kafka's stories were unusual.	
3	Hachiko loved his owner, Mr Ueno, very much.	
4	Mr Ueno's dog waited to meet him at home every day.	
5	'The Hand of the Desert' was created by a famous Chilean sculptor.	

WRITING
A statue in my town

1 Read what Maggie, from Manchester, wrote. Who does she want a statue of and why?

2 Read the text again. Find and <u>underline</u> examples of *was/were* and other verbs in the past simple.

3 Which parts of the text talk about these things? Write 1, 2 or 3 in the boxes.

1 = why the person/people should have a statue
2 = where the writer is from and who the statue is of
3 = what the person/people did

4 Imagine you can choose to have a statue of a famous person (or famous people) in your town/city. Make notes about these things.

1 Where you live.
2 Who the person/people is/are.
3 What the person/people did.
4 Why you think they should have a statue.

5 Write a short text with the title 'A Statue in My Town'.

1 Use Maggie's text to help you.
2 Use your ideas from Exercise 4.
3 Write about 50 words.
4 Check that you used the past simple correctly.

☐ *I live in Manchester in England and I think it's a good idea to have a statue here of a band called The Stone Roses.*

☐ *The band started in 1983 and they only recorded two albums. The first album, in 1989, was a big success. Some people called it 'the best British album of all time'. But the band had some problems and many people didn't like their second album. The band stopped in 1995, but they played more concerts in 2011 and 2012.*

☐ *I think they were important for Manchester because their music helped people all over the world know about the city.*

READING AND WRITING
Part 3: Dialogue matching

1   Complete the conversation between Jim and a waiter. What does Jim say to the waiter?

For questions 1–5, choose the correct letter A–H.

WAITER	Can I help you?
JIM	(0) _____ *E*_____
WAITER	Of course, here you are.

(a few minutes later)

WAITER	Are you ready to order?
JIM	(1) _____
WAITER	Of course. And what would you like to drink?
JIM	(2) _____
WAITER	Would you like dessert?
JIM	(3) _____
WAITER	Certainly.

(45 minutes later)

WAITER	Was the meal OK?
JIM	(4) _____
WAITER	Can I get you anything else?
JIM	(5) _____
WAITER	Of course.

A   Yes, please. Can I have the apple pie?
B   No, just the bill, please.
C   How much is the pasta?
D   Yes, it was lovely, thank you.
E   Yes, can I have the menu, please?
F   Yes, I am. Can I have the pizza, please?
G   Where's the toilet?
H   An orange juice, please.

Part 9: Guided writing

2   Read the email from your pen friend Luca.

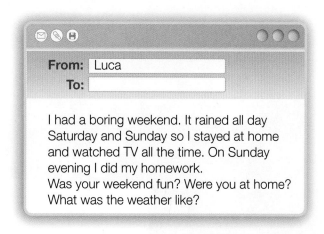

From: Luca
To:

I had a boring weekend. It rained all day Saturday and Sunday so I stayed at home and watched TV all the time. On Sunday evening I did my homework.
Was your weekend fun? Were you at home? What was the weather like?

Write an email to Luca and answer the questions. Write 25–35 words.

TEST YOURSELF

VOCABULARY

1 Complete the sentences with the words in the list. There are two extra words.

at | carrots | cloudy | in | juice | last | meat
oranges | raining | sandwich | warm | yesterday

1   It's a beautiful day today. It's _____ and sunny.
2   Where were you _____ afternoon?
3   I love vegetables; _____ are my favourite.
4   He was born _____ 1994.
5   She arrived _____ half past three.
6   Would you like a chicken and tomato _____ ?
7   It's very _____ today. Perhaps there'll be rain later.
8   There was a lot of rain _____ night.
9   Do you want something to drink? Some _____ , perhaps?
10 No chicken or lamb, thank you. I don't eat _____ .

`/10`

GRAMMAR

2 Complete the sentences with the words in the list.

can | must | mustn't | was | were | would

1   _____ you like eggs for breakfast?
2   It _____ a very windy day yesterday.
3   It's her birthday tomorrow. We _____ remember to say 'Happy Birthday'.
4   _____ we watch TV now, please?
5   Meet me at six o'clock, OK? You _____ be late!
6   There _____ 200 people at the game on Saturday.

3 Find and correct the mistake in each sentence.

1   Last Sunday afternoon we play computer games at home.
2   There was five bananas here this morning. Where are they?
3   I must to do some work tonight.
4   Can I having a cheese salad, please?
5   I tryed to phone you yesterday but there was no answer.
6   I'm thirsty. I like some milk, please.

`/12`

FUNCTIONAL LANGUAGE

4 Complete the missing words.

1   A   Do you want some h _ _ _ with your homework?
    B   No, t _ _ _ _ _ _ , I'm OK.
2   A   Where were you y _ _ _ _ _ _ _ _ _ afternoon?
    B   I w _ _ at home. Why?
3   A   Can you o _ _ _ the window, please?
    B   Yes, of c _ _ _ _ _ _ .
4   B   C _ _ I use your phone, please?
    B   Sure, no p _ _ _ _ _ _ _ .

`/8`

OBJECTIVES

FUNCTIONS: asking and answering about past holidays; talking about ability in the past; describing a picture; sequencing (in a story)

GRAMMAR: past simple: irregular verbs; past simple (negative and questions); *could / couldn't*

VOCABULARY: verb and noun pairs; adjectives

READING

1 Match the words in the list with the photos. Write 1–12 in the boxes.

1 bear | 2 bird | 3 cat | 4 cow | 5 dog
6 elephant | 7 gorilla | 8 horse | 9 tiger
10 rabbit | 11 sheep | 12 snake

2 Complete the sentences with (plural) animals. Then compare your ideas with other students. Use the animals from Exercise 1 or any others that you know.

0 Sometimes _snakes_ are dangerous.
1 Sometimes you see _____ in people's houses.
2 You can find _____ in towns.
3 You can find _____ in the countryside.
4 I like _____ .
5 I don't like _____ .
6 You can find _____ on a farm.
7 _____ can sometimes run very fast.
8 You can find _____ in Africa.
9 People sometimes eat _____ .

3 🔊 2.39 Look at the photos on page 103. What do you think the article is about? Read, listen and check.

4 Read the article again. Choose the correct words.

0 Erin (worked) / was on holiday in Glacier Park.
1 The people wanted to *see bears / have a nice horse ride*.
2 Erin and the boy were on *the same horse / different horses*.
3 The boy's horse ran away because *it / the boy* was scared.
4 *Tonk / Erin* didn't want to move.
5 The boy *fell off / stayed on* the horse's back.
6 *Erin / Erin and Tonk* ran at the bear three times.
7 Erin and Tonk *saved / didn't save* the boy from the bear.

Erin and Tonk to the rescue

Erin Bolster and Tonk

Erin Bolster was a guide in Glacier Park in Montana, USA. In July 2011, she took a group of eight people on horses for a ride in the woods. Erin was on a big white horse called Tonk.

Everyone was ready to have fun, and the ride started well. Erin knew there were bears in the woods, but they didn't usually go near people.

Suddenly, an angry, 300 kilogram grizzly bear came out from the trees. It was very near to an eight-year-old boy who was on his horse. The boy's horse saw the bear and got very scared. It ran away with the boy on its back. The bear ran after them.

Tonk was scared, too. He didn't want to move. But Erin needed to help the boy. She didn't stop to think. She gave Tonk a kick and they went after the bear.

She found the bear near the boy and his horse. Then the boy fell off the horse and the bear started to go towards him! Erin put Tonk between the bear and the boy. Together they ran at the bear three times. The bear made a terrible noise – but then it went away. Erin picked the boy up and took him back to his father and the other riders.

The boy's father was very happy and Erin and Tonk were heroes!

■ THiNK VALUES ■

Animals and us

1 **After Erin and Tonk saved the boy, Erin decided to buy Tonk. Why, do you think? Choose an answer.**

A Tonk didn't have a place to live.
B Erin thought Tonk was a hero.
C Tonk was very cheap.
D Erin thought Tonk was a beautiful horse.

2 **Tick (✓) the things you agree with.**

- [ ] It's important to be nice to animals.
- [ ] Animals and people can live together.
- [ ] It isn't good to eat animals.
- [ ] It isn't good to use animals for clothes.
- [ ] All animals are important.
- [ ] Zoos are bad for animals.
- [ ] Zoos help people understand animals.
- [ ] It isn't good to have animals in your house.

3 **SPEAKING Work in pairs. Compare your ideas with a partner.**

GRAMMAR
Past simple: irregular verbs

1 Look at these examples from the article on page 103. Find the past tense of the other verbs in article and write them in the table.

Erin **put** Tonk between the bear and the boy. Together they **ran** at the bear three times.

1 put	*put*	7 give	
2 run	*ran*	8 go	
3 come		9 know	
4 fall		10 make	
5 find		11 see	
6 get		12 take	

2 Complete the sentences with the past simple form of the words in the list. Use the irregular verbs list on page 128 of the Workbook to help you.

come | drink | eat | fall | forget | get
give | ~~go~~ | run | see | take | write

0 Last weekend we ___went___ to Scotland. My uncle _____ with us.

1 We _____ some nice places and _____ lots of photographs.

2 The little girl _____ too fast and she _____ over.

3 I _____ some good presents for my last birthday. My parents _____ me a bicycle!

4 I _____ an email to my friend but I _____ to send it!

5 My friends and I went to a fast food place last night. We _____ pizza and we _____ milkshakes.

Past simple (negative)

3 These sentences are not true. Use the text on page 103 to correct them. Then choose the correct words to complete the rule.

0 Bears usually went near people.
Bears didn't usually go near people.

1 Tonk wanted to move.

2 Erin stopped to think.

> **RULE:** To make negative sentences in the past simple, we use *didn't (did not)* + the ¹*base / past* form of the verb.
>
> It's ²*the same / different* for both regular and irregular verbs.
>
> It's ³*the same / different* for all subjects (I/you/they/we/he/she/it).

4 Make the sentences negative.

0 I liked the film.
I didn't like the film.

1 I saw my friend at the party.

2 We had a good time.

3 I took a photograph.

4 Our friends came to see us.

5 She found her phone.

Workbook page 100

VOCABULARY
Verb and noun pairs

1 Choose the correct words in the sentences from the text on page 103.

1 Everyone was ready to *have / do* fun.

2 The bear *did / made* a terrible noise.

3 The boy's horse saw the bear and *got / did* very scared.

2 Write the phrases in the correct columns. You can write some phrases in more than one column.

~~a break~~ | a good time | a mistake | a noise
a shower | angry | away | excited | homework
on holiday | photographs | something

have	take	make
	a break	
do	get	go

3 In which column(s) can you add the words in the list? Can you add more words to the columns?

a bath | a party | a train | breakfast | fun | skiing

4 Complete the sentences so they are true for you. Use a positive or negative verb form.

1 I _____ breakfast this morning.

2 I _____ my homework last night.

3 Last weekend, I _____ a lot of photographs with my phone.

4 I _____ a good time at the weekend.

5 My family _____ on holiday last year.

6 The last time I went to a party, I _____ fun.

5 **SPEAKING** Compare your answers with a partner.

Workbook page 103

LISTENING

1 ◀)) 2.40 It's the end of the summer holidays. Ian meets Becky and asks about her holiday. Listen and tick (✓) the correct options.

1 Where did Becky go?

2 Where did she stay?

3 What did she see on her holiday?

  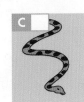

2 ◀)) 2.40 Listen again and choose the correct answers.

1 Where did Becky's dad work in the past?
   A in Belize
   B in a zoo
   C in a shop for animals

2 What animals did Becky's family want to see?
   A snakes
   B birds
   C big cats

3 What did they hear outside?
   A jaguars
   B strange noises
   C other people

■ THiNK SELF-ESTEEM ■
Animals and nature

Tick (✓) the statements that are true for you.

☐ I like camping.
☐ It's exciting to be near animals and nature.
☐ I only want to see animals in a zoo.
☐ I don't like dangerous animals or places.

GRAMMAR
Past simple (questions)

1 Complete the questions from the listening. Write the same word in each space. Then complete the rule.

1 _____ you have a good holiday?
2 _____ you see one?
3 Where _____ you stay, then?
4 What _____ you do on your holiday?

> **RULE:** To form past simple questions, we use
> 1 _____ + I/you/he/she/it/we/they + the base form of the verb.

2 Put the words in order to make questions.

0 to the party / did / go / you ?
   Did you go to the party?
1 she / a good time / did / have ?
2 watch / on TV / did / that programme / you ?
3 they / a lot of / take / photographs / did ?
4 what / for breakfast / did / have / you ?
5 did / you / where / last night / go ?

3 Complete the dialogues.

0 A What _did you watch_ on TV last night?
   B I watched a really good film.
1 A Where _____ on Saturday?
   B I went to the cinema.
2 A What _____ at the zoo?
   B We saw some really cool animals!
3 A What _____ in Italy?
   B We ate spaghetti and pizza.

4 **SPEAKING** Work in pairs. Write questions to ask your partner about their last holiday. Then ask and answer.

... go?   *... stay?*   *... do?*   *... a good time?*

... photographs?   *... on your own?*

Workbook page 101 ➤

Pronunciation
Past simple irregular verbs
Go to page 121.

READING

1 Look at the pictures. These animals don't exist today; they're extinct. Match them with the names in the text. Write 1–3 in the boxes.

2 ◀))2.43 Read and listen to the article. Where did these animals live?

Extinct animals

1 The dodo

The dodo was a bird. It lived on the island of Mauritius, in the Indian Ocean. At one time there were thousands of them on the island. Then people from Europe arrived and started to eat them. The Europeans took animals such as dogs and cats to the island, and the animals ate the dodo eggs. So, why didn't the dodo fly away from the people? Because it couldn't fly. And in 1681, it became extinct.

2 The sabre-toothed cat

This dangerous cat lived thousands of years ago, in North and South America. It had two very big teeth that it used to kill animals. You could see these teeth even when the cat's mouth was closed. People think that this cat could kill very big animals. It became extinct around 10,000 BCE because there wasn't enough food for it.

3 The woolly rhinoceros

This very big animal lived in the middle of Europe and Asia until about 8,000 BCE. It had two horns – the big one was sometimes one metre long. It had a thick woolly coat, so it could keep warm in the cold winters. But then the weather changed a lot and the woolly rhinoceros couldn't live in the warm weather. Also, many people killed them for food. So they died out.

3 Read the article again. Write the names.

0 This animal became extinct when the weather changed.
   woolly rhinoceros

1 These animals became extinct because of people.

   _____   _____

2 This animal killed other animals.

   _____

3 This animal was a bird but it couldn't fly.

   _____

4 This animal was the first to become extinct.

   _____

5 This animal was the last to become extinct.

   _____

GRAMMAR
could / couldn't

1 Complete the examples from the text on page 106. Then read the rule.

1 This cat _____ kill very big animals.
2 The woolly rhinoceros _____ live in the warm weather.

> **RULE:** We use *could*/*couldn't* + the base form of a verb to talk about ability in the past.

2 Use *could*/*couldn't* and a verb from the list to complete the sentences.

~~do~~ | drive | play | ride | see | speak

0 The homework last night was very difficult. I __*couldn't do*__ it! ✗
1 My grandmother _____ without her glasses. ✗
2 My brother _____ the guitar when he was only seven. ✓
3 I _____ a bicycle when I was four. ✓
4 My father _____ a car until he was 25. ✗
5 My grandfather was amazing; he _____ five languages. ✓

3 **SPEAKING** Work in pairs. Think about what you could or couldn't do when you were five. Use the ideas in the list. Add your own ideas.

dance
read and write
ride a bicycle
speak English
swim
take photographs
use a tablet

> When I was five, I couldn't ride a bicycle.

> When I was five, I could swim.

Workbook page 101

VOCABULARY
Adjectives

1 🔊2.44 Write a word from the list under each picture. There are six extra words you don't need. Listen and check.

beautiful | boring | clean | clever
dangerous | dirty | horrible | interesting
lovely | safe | stupid | ugly

2 Match the adjectives and their opposites from Exercise 1.

boring — interesting

3 **SPEAKING** Work in pairs or in small groups. Use the adjectives from Exercise 1 to talk about these things.

your town | a TV programme
a famous person | an animal on TV
a sport that is popular in your country
a famous actor | a place in your country

Workbook page 103

1 _____

2 _____

3 _____

4 _____

5 _____

6 _____

The spider

1 **Look at the photos and answer the questions.**

What do you think Ruby is scared of?
Is Dan nice or horrible to Ruby?

2 🔊 2.45 **Now read and listen to the photostory. Check your answers.**

TOM I had a really good time yesterday.
DAN Yeah? What did you do?
TOM I took the dog for a walk in the forest. It was really fun.
ELLIE That sounds nice.

1

2

ELLIE What about you, Ruby? What did you do yesterday?
TOM Ruby? What's the matter? Did something bad happen?
RUBY Yes. Oh, it was horrible. I don't want to talk about it.
TOM Come on, Ruby. We're your friends. What happened?

RUBY Well, last night I went into my bedroom, and suddenly I saw ... oh, it's stupid.
ELLIE What, Ruby? What? Tell us!
RUBY All right. I sat down and there was a spider on my bed, right beside me! A big, fat, ugly spider.
ELLIE Poor you!
DAN Ha, ha, ha, ha! You're afraid of spiders? I don't believe it!
ELLIE Dan! Don't be horrible! Don't say things like that.
RUBY I hate spiders, Dan! I'm really, really afraid of them!

3

4

TOM That wasn't very nice, Dan. Tell her you're sorry.
DAN Oh, come on. It's silly to be scared of spiders.
TOM But she's really angry with you now.
DAN I've got a great idea, Tom! Let's play a joke on her.
TOM Oh, no! Don't look at me!

DEVELOPING SPEAKING

3 ▶️ EP6 **Watch to find out how the story continues.**

1 What does Dan do to Ruby?

2 What has Jason got?

4 ▶️ EP6 **Watch again. Put the events in order. Write 1–7 in the boxes.**

☐	a	Ellie has got an idea.
☐	b	Ellie talks to a boy called Jason.
☐	c	Jason and Ellie go and talk to Dan.
☐	d	Tom says he's scared of Ellie.
☐	e	Dan gets scared when he looks in Jason's box.
1	f	Dan plays a trick on Ruby with a plastic spider.
☐	g	Dan tells Ruby that he knows how she feels.

PHRASES FOR FLUENCY

1 **Find the expressions 1–4 in the story. Who says them?**

1 What happened?

2 All right.

3 … suddenly …

4 Poor you!

2 **How do you say the expressions in Exercise 1 in your language?**

3 **Put the sentences in the correct order to make a dialogue.**

☐	ANDY	It's true. I was so scared I jumped on the chair and fell off!
☐	ANDY	Because I saw a big, scary spider!
1	ANDY	Can I tell you what happened yesterday?
☐	ANDY	I was in the kitchen, and suddenly, I fell off my chair.
☐	GINA	What? You saw a spider and fell off your chair?
☐	GINA	All right. What happened?
☐	GINA	Oh, poor you! But why?

4 **Complete the dialogues with the expressions from Exercise 1.**

0 A You look really happy! *What happened?*

B I got my test results. 95%!

1 A I think I'm ill.

B _____ ! Perhaps you should stay in bed today.

2 A Julia was horrible last night.

B I know. At first she was OK, but _____ she got angry with me!

3 A There's a great new online computer game. Can I play it, Dad?

B _____ , but only for ten minutes. You've got homework.

FUNCTIONS
Sequencing (in a story)

1 **Read the blog entry. The writer is an animal. Choose which animal the writer is.**

a bird   b cow   c cat

A day in the life of an animal

Home | About | Contact

Today I woke up early, at 05.00. First, I drank some water. Then the farmer came and took the milk. I gave the farmer a kick – ha, ha! I enjoyed that. After that, we went outside. It was a horrible day – very rainy. But we sat in the field. I talked to my friends but they didn't say anything interesting. Later, I ate some grass. Finally, it got dark and we all went home. It was the same as every other day, really!

2 **Find the words and phrases which tell us when things happened and the order in which they happened.**

WRITING
A day in the life of an animal

1 **Choose an animal. Choose from the animals on page 102, or think of a different one.**

Think about:

- what this animal usually does every day
- what the animal eats and drinks
- where the animal goes

2 **Write a blog entry for the animal. Don't write what animal it is! Use the past simple and sequencing words and phrases. Write about 35–50 words.**

3 **Give your blog entry to a partner. Can he/she guess which animal it is?**

A

B

C 1

D

E

READING

1 Match the words in the list with the photos. Write 1–5 in the boxes.

1 a bike | 2 a boat | 3 a bus

4 a car | 5 an underground train

2 **SPEAKING** Work in pairs. When do you use the types of transport in Exercise 1?

> I go to my friend's house by bike.

> I go to school by bus.

3 Put the types of transport in Exercise 1 in order of speed: 1 = slow, 5 = fast.

4 ◁))2.46 Read and listen to the article and write the type of transport under the medal it would win.

 1st

 3rd

 2nd

4th

1 _____

2 _____

3 _____

4 _____

5 Read the article again and match the questions with the answers.

0 Why did the TV show presenters have a race? ___d___

1 Why did they choose different types of transport? ____

2 Why was the result a surprise? ____

3 Why were the presenters unhappy? ____

4 What did the presenters say about the bike? ____

5 Why is the bike a good form of transport in a city? ____

a To find the best one.

b Because the car didn't win.

c Because it is a cheap, clean and healthy form of transport.

d To find the best way to get across London.

e It was dangerous.

f Because the bike won.

A lot of big cities, like London, have got many traffic problems. Sometimes a journey of a few kilometres can take more than an hour. So what's the best way to get across London? For a very short journey, it's probably a good idea to walk. But what happens when you want to go further?

The presenters of a popular TV car show decided to find out. Each of the presenters chose a different type of transport to make the same 27-kilometre journey. One presenter went by bike. One went by car. Another chose public transport – the underground and the bus – and the last one travelled by speedboat up the River Thames. They all started at the same time and the same place in West London, but who got to City Airport in East London first?

The results were a surprise. The bike came first. In second place was the speedboat. Public transport came third and the car was last.

So the presenters had an answer. The bike was quicker than all the other types of transport and the car was slower. They weren't very happy with the result because they wanted the car to win. They made a joke and said the bike wasn't a real winner because it was more dangerous.

But, of course, the bike is the real winner. It's the best way to get about. It's cheaper than public transport and healthier for you than a car. It's also better for our cities because bikes don't pollute the air. So next time you need to go into town, think before you and your parents get into the car – 'Can we make this journey by bike?'

■ THiNK VALUES ■

Transport and the environment

1 **Choose the title that best sums up the article.**

a Cars are great

b The great race

c Get on your bike

d Be careful on your bike

2 **How friendly to the environment do you think these types of transport are? Write 1–6 in the boxes: 1 = best, 6 = worst.**

bus
bike
car
motorbike
plane
train

3 **SPEAKING Work in pairs. Compare your answers with a partner.**

I think number 1 is a bike.

I don't. I think number 1 is a train.

VOCABULARY
Transport

1 🔊 2.47 Match the words in the list with the photos. Write 1–6 in the boxes. Listen and check.

1 ferry | 2 helicopter | 3 motorbike
4 plane | 5 taxi | 6 train

 A 1

 B ☐

 C ☐

 D ☐

 E ☐

 F ☐

2 Look at the photos in Exercise 1 and answer the questions.

Which types of transport travel …

1 on roads?

2 on rails?

3 on water?

4 in the air?

3 **SPEAKING** Can you add any other types of transport to the lists?

Workbook page 111

GRAMMAR
Comparative adjectives

1 Look at the article on page 111. Tick the sentence that isn't true. Then complete the table and the rule.

1 Bikes are *cheaper than* public transport. ☐

2 Bikes are *healthier* for you *than* cars. ☐

3 Cars are *more dangerous than* bikes. ☐

4 Bikes are *better than* other types of transport. ☐

adjective	comparative	
quick	quicker	
big	bigger	
cheap	1 _____	
easy	easier	than
healthy	2 _____	
expensive	more expensive	
dangerous	3 _____	
good	4 _____	

RULE:

● Short adjectives: We usually add -er.
If the adjective ends in consonant + -y, change the y to ¹_____ , e.g. *easy – easier*.
If the adjective ends in vowel + consonant, double the consonant, e.g. *big – bigger*.

● Long adjectives: We add the word ²_____ before the adjective.

● Irregular adjectives: We use a different word, e.g. *good – better, bad – ³_____* .

● After comparative adjectives we use *than*.

2 Write the comparative form of these adjectives.

1 exciting   4 happy   7 funny
2 slow   5 safe   8 hot
3 difficult   6 small   9 fast

3 Look at the types of transport on this page. Write four sentences to compare them.
Planes are quicker than ferries.

4 **SPEAKING** Work in pairs. Read your sentences to your partner, but don't say one of the types of transport. Your partner guesses what it is.

They are quicker than buses.   *Cars!*

Workbook page 108

Pronunciation
Word stress – comparatives
Go to page 121. 🔊

LISTENING

1 ◀)) 2.50 **Amy wants to travel to Brighton. She's at the train station. Listen to the conversation and complete the details of her journey.**

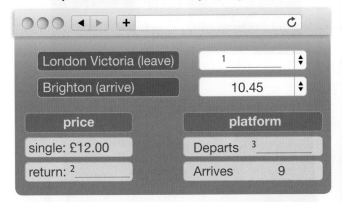

London Victoria (leave)	1 _____
Brighton (arrive)	10.45

price	platform
single: £12.00	Departs 3 _____
return: 2 _____	Arrives 9

2 ◀)) 2.50 **Listen again and answer the questions.**

1 Why doesn't Amy want to take the 9.40 train to Brighton?
2 When does Amy want to return to London?
3 Where is platform 13?
4 Who wants to meet Amy in Brighton?

FUNCTIONS

At the train station

1 **Look at these sentences. Who says them? Write SA (sales assistant) or C (customer) in the boxes.**

0	How can I help you?	SA
1	What time is the next train to London?	
2	What time does the 11.30 arrive in Brighton?	
3	How much is a ticket to Brighton?	
4	Do you want a single or a return?	
5	That's £16.40, please.	
6	What platform does the train leave from?	
7	Have a good journey.	

2 **SPEAKING** **Work in pairs. Use this information and prepare a similar dialogue. Act out your dialogue.**

Chester (leave)	
11.00	11.15

Liverpool (arrive)	
11.45	12.00

price	platform
single: £6.80	5
return: £7.10	5

■ TRAIN TO THiNK ■

Comparing

1 **Write the words in the list in the correct place in the diagram.**

cheap | dangerous | drive | engine | healthy
lights | quick | radio | ride | wheels

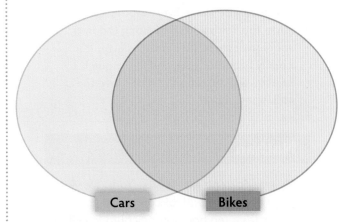

Cars   Bikes

2 **Think of more words to add to the diagram.**

3 **SPEAKING** **Work in pairs. Compare the two forms of transport. Use comparative adjectives.**

> *In London, bikes are quicker than cars.*

READING

1 🔊 2.51 **Read and listen to the magazine article. Write the names under the photos.**

Connor | Julia | Miriam | Nathan

_____

_____

_____

_____

My **favourite** journey

Connor

Every year my family goes on holiday to a small town by the sea. It's got really beautiful beaches and we always have a great time. I love the journey there. We always go by train. It takes about four hours but I don't mind the time. I'm always so excited. I just love watching the mountains and forests go past.

Julia

What's my favourite journey? Any one with my mum on her motorbike. I don't care where we go, I just love being on her bike. She's a really good rider and I always feel safe. I love the wind on my face as we ride through the countryside.

Miriam

My favourite journey is my walk to school. We live on a farm and my school is about one kilometre away. Every morning I walk across the fields and then along the river until I'm at my school in the village. It's a really beautiful walk and it's so quiet. I love my walk to school ... but I love the walk home more!

Nathan

My grandparents live in New York. We visit them every year and, of course, we go by plane. It's a ten hour journey but I love it. I love travelling by plane. It's so exciting. I never get bored because there are lots of films to watch. They always have really good ones.

2 **Read the article again. Correct the information in these sentences.**

0 Connor's family always go to ~~a different~~ place on holiday.
   the same
1 Connor's train journey takes six hours.
2 Julia loves riding on the back of her dad's motorbike.
3 Miriam likes her walk to the local shop.
4 She likes the walk to school more than the walk home.
5 Nathan's aunt and uncle live in New York.

GRAMMAR
one / ones

1 **Look at the examples from the article on page 114. What do the words *one* and *ones* refer to? Then complete the rule with *plural* and *singular*.**

1 What's my favourite journey? Any **one** with my mum on her motorbike.

2 I never get bored because there are lots of films to watch. They always have really good **ones**.

> **RULE:** To avoid repeating a noun, we often use **one** in place of [1]_____ nouns and **ones** in place of [2]_____ nouns.

2 **Write *one* or *ones* in the spaces to replace the crossed out words.**

0 A Do you want to watch this film?
  B No, I've seen that ~~film~~ __one__ before.

1 A Do you want to try on these jeans?
  B No, I'd like to try on the ~~jeans~~ _____ behind them.

2 A What bus can we take?
  B Any ~~bus~~ _____ that's got 'Liverpool' on the front of it.

3 I've got three children. The oldest ~~child~~ _____ is a boy and the younger ~~children~~ _____ are girls.

4 There's a bank in the High Street and there's another ~~bank~~ _____ in Foregate Street.

5 I've got lots of books but my favourite ~~books~~ _____ are my bird books.

Workbook page 109

VOCABULARY
Geographical places

1 **Complete the words with the first and last letters. Use the article on page 114 to help you.**

2 **SPEAKING** **Work in pairs.**

Make a list of famous …
a beaches.
b rivers.
c seas.
d lakes.

3 **Think about your favourite journey. Make notes.**

Where to	
How	
Who with	

4 **SPEAKING** **Tell your partner about your journey.**

> My favourite journey is to the mountains to ski.

> We go by car.

> I go there with my family.

Workbook page 111

0 _m_ ountai _n_

1 __ eac __

2 __ ive __

3 __ e __

4 __ iel __

5 __ ak __

6 __ ar __

7 __ ores __

Culture

Transport around the world

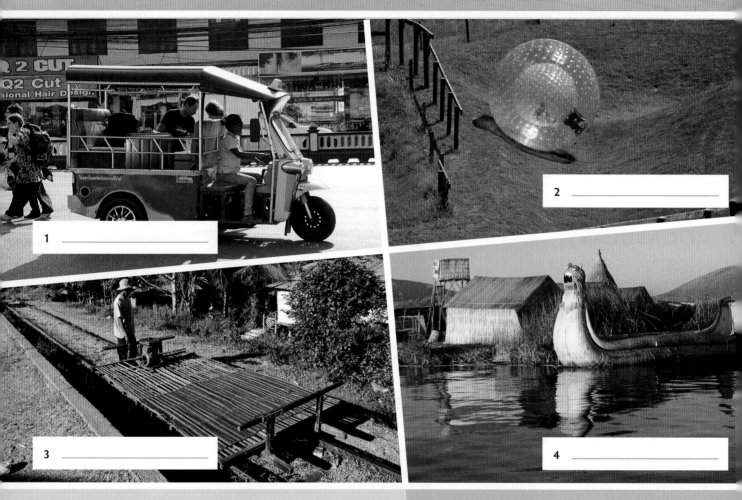

1 _____

2 _____

3 _____

4 _____

The bamboo train, Cambodia

This simple train is made from pieces of bamboo. Local people use it to travel and move things from one village to another. It's got an engine on it and wheels from old trains. It uses the same rails as the national trains and it's a quick way to travel. But be careful: when you hear a train coming, get out of the way quickly!

The zorb, New Zealand

The zorb is not really a type of transport but it is a fun way of getting about. The zorb is a big plastic ball. One person gets inside and the zorb then rolls down the hill. There's a cushion of air to protect the person. It's an exciting way of getting down a hill but it isn't so good for getting up again!

The tuktuk, Thailand

Tuktuks are originally from Thailand, but they are popular in many Asian countries. They've got three wheels and an engine. The noise the engine makes gives the tuktuk its name. They are big enough for two to four people and a suitcase and they are often used for making short trips across busy cities. They're small so they can go through the crowded streets quickly. The journey is often a little dangerous but always exciting.

The totora boat, Peru

Lake Titicaca is a large lake between Peru and Bolivia. The Uro people live in floating villages on the water. They use a local reed called totora to build their homes and boats. The Totora boats are light but very strong. The Uro people build the boats to look like dragons to protect them and their homes.

1 Look at the photos on page 116. Find these things.

a hill | a suitcase | an engine | bamboo | reed | floating villages

2 ◀)) 2.52 Read and listen to the article and write the name of the transport under the pictures.

3 Read the article again and tick (✓) the boxes.

	bamboo train	tuktuk	zorb	totora boat
1 It's got an engine.				
2 It's got wheels.				
3 It travels on water.				
4 It can be dangerous.				
5 It's exciting.				

4 **SPEAKING** Work in pairs. Discuss the questions.

1 Which of these types of transport would you most like to travel on?

2 Are there any unusual types of transport in your country? Where?

WRITING
Unusual forms of transport

1 Read the text. What's the name of the vehicle?

2 Read the text again and answer the questions.

1 Where is it found?

2 Who uses it?

3 What type of transport is it?

4 Why is it unusual?

3 Choose one of these unusual types of transport or one you already know about. Look on the Internet for information. Make notes to answer the questions in Exercise 2.

The Underground Funicular, Istanbul

The Ice Angel, Wisconsin

The Hovercraft, Isle of Wight

4 Use your notes to write a short text about that form of transport. Write 35–50 words.

Amsterdam

Amsterdam is the capital city of Holland. It's a popular city for tourists and it's often quite crowded in the summer months. It's also got a lot of canals so getting about by bus or car is often difficult. *The Flying Dutchman* is a new way of getting about the city. It's an amphibious bus. That means that it's a bus that can go on the roads but it can also travel on the water like a boat. At the moment, *The Flying Dutchman* offers short tours of the city for passengers waiting at the International airport.

■ THiNK EXAMS ■

READING AND WRITING
Part 7: Open cloze

1 **Complete the message left on a holiday blog. Write ONE word in each space.**

Every year my family goes **(0)** ___on___ holiday to a small town by the sea. My grandparents live there. It's **(1)** _____ really beautiful beaches. My favourite one is just next **(2)** _____ their house. I love the journey there. We always go **(3)** _____ train. It's quicker **(4)** _____ the car. It takes about three hours but I don't **(5)** _____ the time. I **(6)** _____ always so excited. I just love watching **(7)** _____ mountains and forests go past. I take lots **(8)** _____ photos of them from the train window. I also play games **(9)** _____ my brother and my parents. We always have **(10)** _____ lot of fun.

LISTENING
Part 3: Three-option multiple choice

2 🔊 2.53 **Listen to Polly talking to her friend Seth about their pets. For each question choose the right answer (A, B or C).**

0 Spot is

  A Polly's dog.   B Seth's dog.   Ⓒ Seth's mum's dog.

1 Flopsie is a

  A rabbit.   B cat.   C dog.

2 Polly's pet is a

  A rabbit called Nemo.   B fish called Nemo.   C cat called Nemo.

3 Nemo eats once a

  A day.   B week.   C month.

VOCABULARY

1   Complete the sentences with the words in the list. There are two extra words.

did | do | farm | forest | fun | get | go
had | horrible | motorbike | safe | taxi

1   That beach is dirty and ugly. I think it's _____ .
2   Let's have some _____ this weekend. How about going to the mountains?
3   We went to London last weekend and we _____ a really good time.
4   There are lots of animals on that _____ .
5   It's snowing! Let's _____ skiing this afternoon.
6   Dangerous? No, it's completely _____ , I promise.
7   Sunday was really boring. I just _____ my homework and nothing else.
8   I don't think it's a good idea to ride a _____ in a big city.
9   It's not really important. Please don't _____ angry about it.
10 We missed the train so we took a _____ to get home.

/10

GRAMMAR

2   Complete the sentences with the words in the list.

better | couldn't | did | good | more | ones | went

1   I was ill, so I _____ go to your party, sorry.
2   Blue? No thanks, I like the red _____ over there.
3   I love this song. It's really _____ .
4   _____ you have fun last weekend?
5   My new phone was _____ expensive than my old one.
6   This film is _____ than her last one.
7   I couldn't go to the concert, but my friends _____ .

3   Find and correct the mistake in each sentence.

1   Are these your new shoes, or are they the old one?
2   My parents gave me this book for my birthday.
3   The chicken was horrible so I not ate it.
4   Went you to the cinema last weekend?
5   I like this shirt because it's cheaper as the other one.
6   I'm bad at French, but Jack is more bad!
7   Did you saw any good films last week?

/14

FUNCTIONAL LANGUAGE

4   Complete the words.

1   A   Hi. Can I have a t _ _ _ _ _ to Manchester, please?
    B   OK. S _ _ _ _ _ _ or r _ _ _ _ _ _ ?
2   A   What time is the n _ _ _ train to Birmingham, please?
    B   3.00 – and after that, there's a train at 3.45.
    A   OK. I want the 3.00 train. What platform does it l _ _ _ _ from?
    B   Platform 4. Have a good j _ _ _ _ _ _ _ !

/6

MY SCORE   /30

| 22 – 30 |
| 10 – 21 |
| 0 – 9 |

PRONUNCIATION

UNIT 1
/h/ or /w/ in question words

1 🔊 1.18 Read and listen to the questions.

How old are you?
Where are you from?
What's your favourite food?
Who's your favourite football player?
Why do you like him?

2 Say the question words in blue.

3 🔊 1.19 Listen again and repeat. Then practise with a partner.

UNIT 2
Vowel sounds – adjectives

1 🔊 1.27 Read and listen to the dialogue.

TOM   Mum's **hungry**.

JANE   Mum? But why? Why is she **angry**?

TOM   I said Mum's **hungry**. She wants a sandwich.

JANE   Oh, … OK. Well, Dad's **angry**.

TOM   Does he want a sandwich, too?

JANE   No! I said he's **angry**.

2 **Which sounds are different in** *hungry* **and** *angry*? **Say them and make the differences clear.**

3 🔊 1.28 Listen again and repeat. Then practise with a partner.

UNIT 3
this / that / these / those

1 🔊 1.36 Read and listen to the dialogue.

ANNA   Can I have **that** cake, please?

ASSISTANT   **This** one or **that** one?

ANNA   **That** one – the chocolate one.

ASSISTANT   **That's** a fruitcake, but **these** cupcakes are chocolate.

ANNA   Oh! Can I have two of **those**, then?

ASSISTANT   Of course. Here you are.

2 **Say the words** *that, this, those* **and** *these.*

3 🔊 1.37 Listen again and repeat. Then practise with a partner.

UNIT 4
Word stress in numbers

1 🔊 1.47 Read and listen to the dialogue.

TIM   It's my sister's birthday today. She's **thirteen**.

JULIE   **Thirty**! That's old!

TIM   **Thirty**? No! I said, '**Thirteen**'.

JULIE   Oh, … **thirteen**. She's the same age as me.

2 **Where is the stress on the red words? Where is the stress on the blue words?**

3 🔊 1.48 Listen again and repeat. Then practise with a partner.

UNIT 5
Present simple verbs – third person

1 🔊 1.54 Read and listen to the sentences.

Liz **catches** the bus to school every morning.
She **teaches** French at a secondary school.
At 4.30 she **finishes** work.
After dinner, Liz **washes** the dishes.
Before she goes to bed, she **chooses** her clothes for the next day.

2 **How many syllables are there in** *catch*? **How many syllables are there in** *catches*? **Say the words in blue.**

3 🔊 1.55 Listen again and repeat. Then practise with a partner.

UNIT 6
Long vowel sound /eɪ/

1 🔊 1.65 Read and listen to the dialogue.

CUSTOMER   I'm sorry I'm **late**. I have a table for 1.00.

WAITER   That's **okay**. But **Jane Grey's waiting** for you.

CUSTOMER   OK. But I don't know her. Is she the girl there, with the long **straight** hair?

WAITER   No. Her hair's **wavy** and **grey**.

CUSTOMER   Oh! The woman with the pink **face**? The one eating **cake**?

WAITER   Yes, that's her. I'll **take** you to the **table**.

2 **Say the words in blue. Which vowel sound do they all have?**

3 🔊 1.66 Listen again and repeat. Then practise with a partner.

UNIT 7
Long vowel sound /ɔː/

1   🔊 2.03   **Read and listen to the dialogue.**

PAUL   Do you like **sport**?

LAURA   Oh, yes, it's very **important**. I love **skateboarding**.

PAUL   So do I! Are there any **more sports** you like?

LAURA   Well, I like **all ball** games. Hmm … what time is it, **Paul**?

PAUL   It's **quarter** to **four**, Laura.

LAURA   I have to go. I'm playing **football** at **four**.

2   **Say the words in blue. Which vowel sound do they all have?**

3   🔊 2.04   **Listen again and repeat. Then practise with a partner.**

UNIT 8
Intonation – listing items

1   🔊 2.17   **Read and listen to the dialogue.**

MUM   I'm going shopping. Do you want anything?

BRAD   Yes, Mum! I need a T-shirt. Oh, and some socks, please.

MUM   OK. A T-shirt and socks …

BRAD   Actually, I need a T-shirt, socks, trainers, a jacket and a baseball cap.

MUM   A T-shirt, socks, trainers, a jacket and a baseball cap. I think you need to come with me!

2   **Brad wants *a T-shirt, socks, trainers, a jacket* and *a baseball cap*. Circle the arrows to show when his voice goes up and when it goes down.**

3   🔊 2.18   **Listen again and repeat. Then practise with a partner.**

UNIT 9
Intonation – giving two choices

1   🔊 2.26   **Read and listen to the dialogue.**

WAITRESS   Would you like salad or soup?

MIKE   Salad, please.

WAITRESS   Chicken or fish?

MIKE   I think I'll have fish today.

WAITRESS   Would you like dessert?

MIKE   Yes, please!

WAITRESS   Cake or fruit?

MIKE   Hmm … I'll have the fruit.

WAITRESS   And coffee or tea?

MIKE   Oh, coffee, please.

2   🔊 2.27   **Circle the arrows in the dialogue to show when the waitress' voice goes up and when it goes down. Listen and check.**

3   🔊 2.27   **Listen again and repeat. Then practise with a partner.**

UNIT 10
Past simple regular verbs

1   🔊 2.35   **Read and listen to the story.**

My grandmother **lived** in the country. She **walked** to town to go to school. She **finished** school when she was twelve. She **started** working in a bottle factory. She **worked** in the factory until she **married** my grandfather. One day, she **invented** a machine that cleaned bottles. The factory **wanted** the machine and my grandparents were rich after that!

2   **The -ed ending is pronounced differently in the red and blue words. What's the difference?**

3   🔊 2.36   **Listen again and repeat. Then practise with a partner.**

UNIT 11
Past simple irregular verbs

1   🔊 2.42   **Read and listen to the dialogue.**

PETER   **Could** you ride a bike when you were young, Grandma?

GRANDMA   I certainly **could**, Peter. I **went** to school on my bike. I **put** my books in the basket.

PETER   **Could** you swim?

GRANDMA   Of course I **could**!

PETER   **Were** you good?

GRANDMA   I **was** very good! I **swam** across the lake. Look – here's a photo my father **took** when I finished.

PETER   Wow, Grandma. I **couldn't** do that!

2   **Say the past tense words in blue. What is the infinitive form of these verbs?**

3   🔊 2.43   **Listen again and repeat. Then practise with a partner.**

UNIT 12
Word stress – comparatives

1   🔊 2.48   **Read and listen to the sentences.**

A plane is faster than a car.
A bike is slower than a train.
A speedboat is quicker than a ferry.
A bike is easier to ride than a horse.

2   **Find the comparative adjective in each sentence. Which syllable is stressed in each of these words?**

3   🔊 2.49   **Listen again and repeat. Then practise with a partner.**

GET IT RIGHT!

UNIT 1
Be

> Learners often miss out *am*, *are* or *is* in sentences.
>
> **We use the subject + *be* + object.**
> ✓ *I'm from Spain.*
> ✗ *I from Spain.*
>
> **In questions, we use *be* + subject + object + question mark.**
> ✓ *Are they from Scotland?*
> ✗ *They from Scotland?*

Tick ✓ the correct sentences and cross ✗ the incorrect ones. Correct the mistakes.

0   He my favourite athlete.　　　　✗
    He is my favourite athlete.
1   The house very nice.
2   How old you?
3   I'm from Edinburgh.
4   You 13 years old?
5   What your name?
6   My favourite singer is Sam Smith.
7   My name John.
8   Lisbon in Spain?

Subject pronouns and *be*

> Learners sometimes miss out the subject pronoun when using *be*.
>
> **We always use the subject + *be*.**
> ✓ *This is Mike. He is from England.*
> ✗ *This is Mike. Is from England.*

Correct the mistakes in the sentences.

0   I like Maria. Is very funny.
    I like Maria. She is very funny.
1   I like England. Is very nice.
2   It's a taxi. Is yellow.
3   She's my friend. Is from Mexico.
4   They are singers. Are in First Aid Kit.
5   He's my brother. Is 15 years old.
6   I like this phone because is very small.

UNIT 2
Be questions

> Learners make mistakes with word order in *be* questions.
>
> **In positive sentences, we use subject + *be*. In questions, we use the order *be* + subject + (object) followed with a question mark (?).**
> ✓ *That is OK.*
> ✓ *Is that OK?*
> ✗ *That is OK?*

Put the words in the correct order to make questions.

0   it / expensive / is ?
    Is it expensive?
1   there / is / problem / a ?
2   on / holiday / are / you ?
3   how / you / are ?
4   a / is / famous person / he ?
5   computer game / this / is / your ?
6   she / is / sister / your ?

Spelling

> Learners sometimes have trouble spelling words in English.
> ✓ *That is my pencil.*
> ✗ *That is my pensil.*

Correct the spelling mistakes in the sentences.

0   She is my frind.
    She is my friend.
1   My brother is very funy.
2   The food is excelent.
3   My shirt is withe.
4   We play football in the evining.
5   I saw her yesterday moring.
6   The film is greate.

UNIT 3
Possessive 's

Learners find it difficult to use possessive 's. They often put the words in the wrong order.

We use person + possessive 's + thing/person.

✓ This is my brother's car.
✗ This is ~~the car of my brother~~.

Rewrite the sentences using possessive 's.

0   I went to the house of my cousin.
    I went to my cousin's house.
1   It is the homework of my sister.
2   The name of my friend is Amy.
3   I was at the party of my friend.
4   The family of my friend lives in India.
5   It is the birthday of my sister.
6   This is the bedroom of my brother.
7   Trumpington High is the school of my cousin.
8   Don't eat the burger of Juan!
9   That's the chair of the teacher.
10 He's the brother of Ana.

Family vocabulary

Learners sometimes make spelling mistakes with family words.

✓ This is my cousin Jean.
✗ This is my ~~cousine~~ Jean.
✗ This is my ~~couzin~~ Jean.

Correct the spelling mistakes in the family words.

0   How is your familly?
    How is your family?
1   My mather is in hospital.
2   We go to my granmother's house.
3   I watch films with my borther.
4   It was a present from my fater.
5   He is the president's sun.
6   He has got two daugthers.
7   My granfather lives there.
8   She is my cousine.
9   His family are form America.
10 Does your uncel live near you?

UNIT 4
There is / There are

Learners sometimes miss out *there* where *there is/are* is required.

We use *there* + *be* + noun, where *be* agrees with the noun. We do not use *there have* or *there has*.

✓ There is a great café on this street.
✗ ~~Is a great café~~ on this street.
✗ ~~There has a great café~~ on this street.

Correct the mistakes in the sentences.

0   Next week is a party.
    Next week there is a party.
1   In the kitchen are two windows.
2   In Paris there has a nice park.
3   Are any other drinks?
4   In my room there has a bed.
5   It is nice because are lots of shops.
6   Near my town there have lots of interesting places.

Prepositions of place

Learners sometimes make mistakes with the form of prepositions of place, either misspelling them or using the wrong particle.

✓ The shop is next to the post office.
✗ The shop is ~~next the post office~~.

Correct the mistakes in the sentences.

0   My house is oposite the school.
    My house is opposite the school.
1   The coffee shop is infront of the bank.
2   My house is nex to Park Hotel.
3   I live behing the station.
4   Station Road is beetween the supermarket and the post office.
5   The shop is opposit the museum.
6   Their houses are next the hospital.

UNIT 5
Present simple positive

> **Learners often make agreement mistakes in the present simple.**
>
> ✓ It helps me with my studies.
> ✗ It ~~help~~ me with my studies.

Correct the mistakes in the sentences.

0   He play football.
    He plays football.
1   He eat breakfast every day.
2   They likes sports.
3   She go to university.
4   Angela work Monday to Friday.
5   People plays games on their phones.
6   School start on Friday.
7   People in cities is often angry.
8   He studyies every day after school.
9   She love Glee Club.
10 My brother watchs football on TV every Saturday.

Present simple negative

> **Learners sometimes make agreement mistakes in the present simple negative.**
>
> **The verb *do* agrees with the person and number of the subject.**
>
> ✓ He doesn't like sports.
> ✗ He ~~don't~~ like sports.

Choose the correct options in the sentences.

0   They (don't) / doesn't understand.
1   She *doesn't / don't* have any time.
2   He *doesn't / don't* like sweets.
3   We *doesn't / don't* need to wear tennis clothes.
4   It *don't / doesn't* cost much.
5   My teacher *don't / doesn't* give me a lot of homework.
6   I *don't / doesn't* like computer games.
7   I *don't / doesn't* play sports after school.
8   You *don't / doesn't* go to my school.
9   My brother *don't / doesn't* help me with my homework.
10 Planes *don't / doesn't* fly to our city.

UNIT 6
Countable and uncountable nouns

> **Learners sometimes confuse *a(n)* with *some*.**
>
> **We use *a* or *an* with countable nouns in the singular. We use *some* for countable nouns in the plural.**
>
> ✓ We can buy a present for his birthday.
> ✗ We can buy ~~some present~~ for his birthday.
> ✓ We can buy some presents for his birthday.
>
> **We also use *some* with uncountable nouns.**
>
> ✓ You need some water.
> ✗ You need ~~a water~~.

Choose the correct options in the sentences.

0   I've got *some /* (a) T-shirt.
1   We took a break and ate *some / a* sandwich.
2   The best present was *some / a* jacket.
3   I have got *some / a* good news.
4   Can you take *some / a* photo of us?
5   I listen to *some / a* nice music with my family.
6   He has got *some / a* good friends.

has / have got

> **Learners often forget to include *got* when they use *has / have got* in negative sentences and questions.**
>
> ✓ Has he got a dog?
> ✗ Has he a dog?
> ✓ He hasn't got a bike.
> ✗ He hasn't a bike.

Correct the mistakes in the sentences

0   I haven't any sisters
    I haven't got any sisters
1   Have you the time?
2   Has your mum GPS in her car?
3   I haven't headphones. Can I use yours?
4   They haven't books in their school. They use tablets.
5   I haven't an e-reader. I use my phone.
6   Have you a laptop?

UNIT 7
can / can't

Learners sometimes use the wrong form of the verb when they use *can* and *to*.

We use the infinitive without *to* after *can*.

✓ *He can play the piano.*
✗ *He ~~can to play~~ the piano.*

We use *to* + infinitive after *want* and *need*.

✓ *They want to know the answer.*
✗ *They ~~want know~~ the answer.*

Correct the mistakes in the sentences.

0   He needs do that.
    He needs to do that.
1   Can you to speak Spanish?
2   We want do some shopping.
3   You need clean your room.
4   I need eat something. I'm hungry!
5   I can't to do my homework.
6   Alex wants do everything.

UNIT 8
like / don't like + verb + -ing

Learners sometimes use the wrong form of the verb where *-ing* is required.

We use the *-ing* form of verbs after the verbs *like*, *don't like*, *love* and *hate*.

✓ *I like playing tennis.*
✗ *I ~~like play~~ tennis.*
✗ *I ~~like to playing~~ tennis.*

Correct the mistakes in the sentences.

0   I like read books.
    I like reading books.
1   I like sing and dancing.
2   We love go shopping.
3   She likes to wearing green clothes.
4   They don't like play basketball.
5   Paul doesn't hate study.
6   Anna likes to wearing white clothes.

UNIT 9
must / mustn't / can / would

Learners often have trouble spelling modal verbs *can't*, *must*, *would* and *mustn't*.

Correct the spelling mistakes in the sentences.

0   Wold you like to go with me?
    Would you like to go with me?
1   I cant find the coffee.
2   You mast learn English.
3   I woud like to do some shopping.
4   You musn't use YouTube©.
5   Woudn't you like some more?
6   We mussn't be late.

UNIT 10
was / wasn't, were / weren't

Learners sometimes confuse *was* and *were*.

Was, *wasn't*, *were* and *weren't* all have to agree with the subject.

✓ *The jeans were very beautiful.*
✗ *The jeans ~~was~~ very beautiful.*

Tick ✓ the correct sentences and cross ✗ the incorrect ones. Correct the mistakes.

0   There was a lot of people.   ☒
    There were a lot of people.
1   We was at Dan's house all night.   ☐
2   There was a lot of food.   ☐
3   Wasn't you there?   ☐
4   I were happy to see you at the weekend.   ☐
5   How many people were at your house?   ☐
6   Last night there were a party on the beach.   ☐
7   He was my friend at school.   ☐
8   Katie and Jo was there.   ☐

UNIT 11
Past simple (irregular verbs)

> Learners sometimes use the wrong forms of irregular verbs in the past simple or misspell them.
>
> ✓ *I paid a lot of money.*
> ✗ *I ~~payed~~ a lot of money.*

Correct the mistakes in the sentences.

0   I haved a holiday.
     I had a holiday.
1   I maked a lot of friends.
2   She gived me a lot of presents.
3   Jack and Al taked photographs.
4   There where some problems with his work.
5   I cam home late yesterday.
6   He swimmed very fast.
7   They goed to the cinema.
8   Helen mad some food.

Past simple (negative)

> Learners sometimes use the present simple negative where the past simple is required.
>
> ✓ *I didn't find the answer before the end of the exam.*
> ✗ *I ~~don't~~ find the answer before the end of the exam.*

Choose the correct options.

0   We *don't /* (*didn't*) go to the game last week.
1   I *didn't / don't* need any help at the moment.
2   I bought some T-shirts but I *didn't / don't* buy any tops.
3   I went to a mobile phone shop but I *didn't / don't* like the phones there.
4   Do you like chicken? No, I *didn't / don't* eat meat.
5   I had a lot of presents but he *didn't / don't* give me one.
6   We *didn't / don't* usually go on holiday because we like being at home.

UNIT 12
Comparative adjectives

> Learners often use *more* and *-er* in the same sentence when only one of these forms is required.
>
> We form comparative adjectives by adding *-er* if the adjective has one syllable (or two syllables ending in *-y*), and by using *more* if the adjective has two or more syllables. We don't use *more* and *-er* together.
>
> ✓ *This one is bigger than that one.*
> ✗ *This one is ~~more bigger~~ than that one.*
> ✗ *This one is ~~more big~~ than that one.*

Correct the mistakes in the sentences.

0   The train is more cheap than the plane.
     The train is cheaper than the plane.
1   He is more healthier than he was last year.
2   Henry is more older than his brother.
3   My mobile phone is more newer than my brother's.
4   Basketball is more good than baseball.
5   I was more happy than Joe at the end of the game.
6   Henry's brother is more friendlier than Henry.
7   I think Maths is more easy than English.

than with comparative adjectives

> Learners sometimes use *then* or *that* where *than* is required with comparative adjectives.
>
> ✓ *Colin is older than Oliver.*
> ✗ *Colin is older ~~then~~ Oliver.*
> ✗ *Colin is older ~~that~~ Oliver.*

Complete the sentences with *then*, *that* or *than*.

0   He can run faster __*than*__ me.
1   It is much better _____ your mobile phone.
2   Call me _____ .
3   It is more _____ I thought.
4   _____ is my book.
5   This one is better than _____ one.
6   We danced and _____ watched a film.

STUDENT A

UNIT 4, PAGE 43, VOCABULARY

Student A

Ask and answer the questions with your partner.

> How much is the smartphone?

> It's ...

> How much are the ...?

> They're ...

UNIT 6, PAGE 61, TRAIN TO THINK

Student A

Describe to your partner what the people in your picture look like. Your partner describes what the people in his/her picture look like. Find the six differences.

UNIT 8, PAGE 79, TRAIN TO THINK

Student A

Listen to the questions your partner asks about the picture in Exercise 2. Answer with short answers. Correct the negative answers.

1   Are there ten people in the band?
2   Is the singer wearing a red dress?
3   Are there two guitar players in the band?
4   Are there five trumpet players in the band?
5   Are all the band members wearing hats?

STUDENT B

UNIT 4, PAGE 43, VOCABULARY

Student B

Ask and answer the questions with your partner.

How much is the TV?

It's ...

How much are the ...?

They're ...

UNIT 6, PAGE 61, TRAIN TO THINK

Student B

Describe to your partner what the people in your picture look like. Your partner describes what the people in his/her picture look like. Find the six differences.

UNIT 8, PAGE 79, TRAIN TO THINK

Student B

Listen to the questions your partner asks about the picture in Exercise 2. Answer with short answers. Correct the negative answers.

1 Are there eight people dancing?
2 Are the two dancing women wearing green dresses?
3 Is one dancing man wearing a blue shirt?
4 Are eight people drinking?
5 Are four people sitting down?